A Co-Conspirator's Guide to Thriving (and Surviving) in The Training Game

FROM MY SEAT ON THE BUS

Wit and Wisdom from the Collected Works of

Ron Zemke

Senior Editor of TRAINING Magazine

Compiled and Edited By Dave Zielinski

Bulk reprints of individual articles may be quoted and purchased through:

Reprint Services
315 Fifth Avenue N.W.
St. Paul, MN   55112
(800) 707-7798 or (612) 633-0578

LAKEWOOD BOOKS
50 South Ninth Street
Minneapolis, MN   55402
(800) 707-7769 or (612) 333-0471
Fax: (612) 333-6526
Web Page Address: http: //www.lakewoodpub.com

Editorial Director: Linda Klemstein
Editor: Dave Zielinski
Production Manager: Kimberly Shannon
Cover Design / Production Editor: Julie Tilka
Proofreader: Julie Maas
Illustrator: John Bush

Lakewood Publications Inc. publishes TRAINING Magazine, Presentations Magazine, Training Directors' Forum Newsletter, Creative Training Techniques Newsletter, The Lakewood Report On Technology for Learning Newsletter, Potentials In Marketing Magazine and other business periodicals, books, research, and conducts conferences.

ISBN 0-943210-50-X

10 9 8 7 6 5 4 3 2 1

PREFACE

I found my first job working for someone other than my Dad when I was 15. It was in a barbershop in Sterling, IL. Shining shoes. Sweeping up. Hanging out and getting paid for it, sort of. At the end of that first six-day week I had shined 97 pairs of shoes at 30 cents a pair. The shop owner kept half the gross, and I took home $14.55. The second week on the job I shined 107 pairs of shoes and took home $1.50 — that was the week I learned about coin matching games from the kid who ran the shine stand at the pool hall down the block.

The third week I shined 92 pair and took home $8.50 — that was the week I learned that only dummies believe games of chance are fair.

Week four — 95 pair and $12.25 — I learned about paying for protection. Week five — 97 pair and $17 — I learned that all agreements are open to renegotiation and that sometimes you have to fight back to keep what's yours.

I've been learning about the real rules of working for a living ever since.

Throughout high school, college, graduate school, and the numerous "real" training jobs and consulting gigs since, the same pattern has endured. Live a little, work a little, learn a little and move along. After 40 years of that, I know a lot more than I did when I was 15. Most of all, I know that there is a lot left for me to learn; indeed, for most of us in the training trade to learn — if we're willing to discomfort ourselves a little bit to learn it.

In December 1975 a fellow named Tom Namacher offered me the break of a lifetime. Tom is a genuine, not-to-be-mistaken-for-anything-else entrepreneur who happened to own a publishing company called Lakewood Publications. He and his co-conspirator, Jim Secord, had just purchased a magazine called TRAINING. Tom and his freshly-minted editor, Phil Jones, needed a whole lot of words to fill up the pages of their new magazine, and hadn't a lot of staff or money to do it with. I was a struggling ex-banker cum graduate student with a yen to put words on paper and get paid for it. Lakewood reached out to me, and a partnership was born.

Some 22 years, 300 training articles, and 13 business books later, I'm still struggling to learn how to "write readable" and I'm still learning about life, liberty and the world of work the same way I always have — as I go, one rule at a time.

Most of what is contained in this volume comes from the last seven years of scribbling about the training and development trade for a living. Some of it goes back a little further, but not much. Many of the columns here are about the tumultuous, frightening, exasperating, exhilarating and often-wondrous times we live in. Today's tomorrows are so scary and so promising I sometimes can hardly wait to go to bed so I can get up and unwrap one of them. Always something new to discover. And more than even odds of a nervous breakdown.

I hope you find in these pages some reflections of yourself, your friends, your colleagues, your boss, your ex-boss and any number of people you've bumped into — and up against — working for a living. You and I have probably learned many of the same things. After all, we're all on the same bus, moving down the same highway and through the same scenery, thinking about many of the same things as we go.

But I also hope we've learned a few disparate lessons as well. So here's wishing the view from my seat on the bus is different enough from yours that you'll enjoy my slightly-altered perspective. And here's hoping you'll get something of a kick out of it as well.

Ron Zemke
Minneapolis, MN
November 1996

CONTENTS

CHAPTER ONE: TRENDS IN TRAINING

CHAPTER TWO: THE INFLUENTIAL TRAINING LEADER

CHAPTER THREE: THE OFTEN-STRANGE FASCINATIONS OF HRD FOLK

CHAPTER 1

TRENDS IN TRAINING

INTRODUCTION

Don't Panic:
Only the Wrapping Is New

About 111 years ago, during week one of my first legitimate training management job, I found myself locked in a rancorous meeting over a plan I had for turning an effective, but interminably long course in small business lending into a one-day seminar. My shortened seminar would be preceded by a qualifying self-study routine of programmed instruction, audio tapes, and guided lesson plans.

When we broke for a hygiene break, one of my combatants — Roger, a VP who had seven years earlier authored this behemoth of a course, and who was but 17 days away from his retirement party — leaned toward me and offered this bit of friendly wisdom: "You know, Ron, there is nothing new under the sun."

Then and there I promised myself two things. First, I would avoid at all costs going to the restroom at the same time as someone I was arguing with, and second, if I ever started spouting such Monty Pythonesque Roger-isms, I would either take a vow of silence and repair to a monastery or shoot myself.

But in the intervening years, I have been alarmed and chagrined to learn that if you hang out on the same street corner long enough, you are, in fact, going to experience a lot of what the philosopher/baseball player Yogi Berra called "déjà vu all over again" — and find yourself sorely tempted to start spewing embarrassing aphorisms such as "there is nothing new under the sun" or the equally vapid, "the more things change, the more they stay the same."

So, given the forewarning that I may have indeed fallen under the same spell of that life segment where, like old Roger, I am in desperate need to believe I and my cohort group have made every discovery and solved every training problem "under the sun," let me risk a couple of observations from my seat on the HRD express:

1. Training and development people are, like Los Angeles waiters and New York City cabdrivers, always in the process of becoming something else.

This year it is performance consultants, last year it was multimedia mavens, the year before that reengineering "analysts" and the year before that total quality experts.

This insistence on continually reinventing ourselves to be in step with the latest fad filtering down from the boardroom may be prudent in this time of "job discontinuity" (how's that for a new euphemism?). It certainly demonstrates an eager and easy flexibility, as in:

•"Team building in the Amazon Rain Forest? Great idea Mr. Dithers. I know that Dagwood and the gang would really get a lot out of your brother-in-law's swell program."

•"You'd like me to take over the accounts receivable reengineering task force? No problem, boss. I've always enjoyed those merry pranksters in accounting."

I understand the urge to continually morph to match changing times and top management's whims. I personally have done more flip flops on just what my "thing" is than a carp on the bottom of a bass boat. It might be nice, however, if one of these days we as a profession decide that it's OK to be what we already are, and what we always have been: people who like helping other people learn to do their jobs better, and not worry about defining that only in terms of the latest Dilbert strip or the hottest fad on some business book bestsellers list. There is, I would argue, nothing at all wrong with defining yourself simply in terms of what you do well ... and enjoy doing.

The real harm in continually shedding your old skin is that in the effort to keep up with what is trendy, it is possible to lose one's center — and rob yourself of the satisfaction of being successful at your real competence.

2. Training professionals are a little quick to follow the latest fad.

Our profession is a bit too hasty to pounce on the latest fad like a bald eagle on a trout.

I have no doubt that if some guy with a Ph.D. from Harvard or U.C.L.A. could show us a survey proving that 75 percent of a sample of 12 CEOs who played 11 or more consecutive games of pinball had rated their creativity as "highly enhanced," we'd be out looking or a pinball guru speaker, a "how to" pinball book, and a pinball conference to send our people to. And I'd be fighting with the editors of *TRAINING Magazine* over who gets to write the cover story entitled: "Pinball Creativity: Fad or Fix for Corporate America's Innovation Woes?"

Again, let me emphasize that I am not suggesting we are fickle airheads, or that everything we need to know how to do has already been invented. Far from it. I would suggest, however, that before we start damning management for only being able to see the short term, we look around and assess our own sight-to-the-end-of-our-noses tendencies.

3. T&D people are often more interested in RESPECT than in RESULTS.

As any training consultant can tell you, trying to construct and sell an evaluation or an ROI study to a skeptical senior manager is 30 times more difficult than selling a new communications style instrument or a glitzy new sales training concept. We talk a good game when it comes to proving on-the-job impact and bottom line influence, but when senior management balks at the cost of actually proving the effectiveness of a performance intervention, and puts on the apron and hair net and says, *"We'll* know whether this works or not — run along and play with the other children," we are all too quick to roll up our knickers and head for the sandbox.

That tail-between-the-legs routine may indeed be the only rational thing we can afford to do in this job-insecure world. In doing so we are following a coarse but constant rule: "To thine corporate culture be true, so thy days may be long upon the payroll that feedeth thee." It is prudent to only fight battles that are worth fighting — and that you know you can win.

But respect doesn't come from being the first kid on the block to tell senior management to read "The Habits of Seven Highly Obnoxious People" or from buying the latest integrated multimedia virtual reality cheese slicer or from knowing the most buzzwords. Granted all those things can get you noticed in the organization. But, let's face it, so can painting your posterior red and running around the office singing "Lookie, lookie, I'm a raspberry cookie."

Respect comes not from being a zealot, a fad-follower or from carrying a cross for self-paced multimedia or for ropes-and-ladders training in the wilderness. To paraphrase columnist Jimmy Breslin, "Respect is a funny thing. Whether you think you have it or whether you think you don't....You're right!"

What follows are some simple observations on the universal urge to make change for change sake — and to forever posture different as new or better. Happy fad-busting. — **R.Z.**

Bean Counters in the Information Age

I don't like Robert Half. True, I don't know Robert Half. And the only person I know who ever did meet Robert Half says he is a peach of a guy, a good boss, a natural leader and a pretty fair dancer. You could say I don't like him on a symbolic level.

What I don't like about Robert Half, whose name is on the door of the "world's largest" financial, accounting and data processing recruitment agency, is his apparent conception of what the working world should look like. As expressed by the frequent press releases he sends out, it's a view that seems to peek out from under a green eyeshade at a universe whose boundaries are strictly defined by time clocks and stopwatches — a world that doesn't function properly unless "we're all in our places with sunshiny faces."

One recent example was titled "American Workers Will Steal Over $160 Billion Dollars In Time This Year." It came to my attention courtesy of Robert Half International's New York public relations firm. The point of the press release, which has been picked up and carried by news services and business magazines across the country, is easy to discern from the title. According to Half — or whoever does these strange studies for him — 80% of the American workforce is involved in "time theft." Though that may sound like a rejected plot idea from a Monty Python flick or a *Saturday Night Live* skit, it is not.

> When 'thinking' is the activity that creates greatest value, standards measured by time clocks become inanely obsolete.

Time theft is what you and I are engaged in when we leave early, arrive late, make personal phone calls on company time, socialize with other employees, take care of personal business on company time, read newspapers, books or magazines, listen to the radio on the job, and take too many coffee breaks.

By Half's estimate you and I, on average, steal six workweeks a year from our employers. Aggregated for the national workforce and translated into dollars, that comes to roughly 90% of the annual national debt increase during the Reagan administration.

What raises my ire about this view of an honest day's work is the implication that unless I am tightening lug nuts on an assembly line, waiting tables in an overcrowded, understaffed restaurant, or sitting bolt upright at a terminal, keyboarding mindlessly for eight straight hours, I am a perpetrator of industrial pilferage.

I reject as antediluvian the assumption that a body not in motion is a body willfully nonproductive. That is an industrial-era bean-counter's mentality,

improperly carried forward and grafted badly onto the information age. As a valid productivity measurement strategy, seats-in-seats is a set of calipers being applied to a particle accelerator: It measures nothing. Mindless motion or ciphers-per-minute may once have been acceptable indicators — though not measures of — productivity, but that era is in its dotage.

Today, when more and more of the things we can easily observe and measure in human behavior have at best a trivial relationship to outcome, time and motion studies fail to inform. When thinking — not lifting and carrying — is the activity that most directly creates value, standards measurable by time clocks become inanely obsolete.

I have been in too many marathon meetings where important problems were solved by a serendipitous combination of working the problem, getting off track, telling jokes and goofing-off, to brook criticism of the process as "time theft." I have spent too many important days buried in books and magazines, working quite productively, thank you, to the tunes of Strauss or the Rolling Stones, to agree to a charge of malicious malingering.

I simply cannot buy "management by factory whistle" as an appropriate model for the waning years of the 20th century. What is the substitute? There are 101 candidates. Management by mission. Management by example. Management by incentive. Even management by abdication seems a better bet.

I don't know what to call it yet, but I know it when I see it. I saw it in an interview I did several years ago with a crazy Norwegian named Olaf Isachsen, who, at the time, was vice president of HRD at Wells Fargo Bank. Searching for a way to describe the importance of a supportive sponsor/mentor/boss to a successful HRD effort, he came up with a perfect example. "Just the other day," he said, "[my boss] came into my office and there I sat with my feet up, shoes off, looking across the Bay thinking about something or other. And do you know what he said? He said, 'I'll talk to you later. I didn't know you were working.' That's a real fine understanding of what we're trying to do here."

It's also a real fine illustration of why the bean-counter mentality is a poor framework for managing work in the information age. ∎

Claiming Nickels on The Bottom Line Won't Fulfill Your Training Mission

E xcuse me, but I am bored with the bottom line. I'll make a deal with you; a late New Year's resolution with two signatories — you and me. If you'll expunge the phrase "bottom line" from your vocabulary, I'll ban it from mine.

I have had it with that overworked coupling. There are times when I was sure it must be a violation of some obscure federal regulation to publish a book, write an article, or make a speech in public without invoking the thunderous "IT HAS TO MAKE SENSE ON THE BOTTOM LINE" or one of its shopworn cognates. What a bore. To my mind, it is just a shade short in the hackneyed-phrase department of "people are our most important resource."

Were it only that — a hyperactive hackneyed phrase — I could grit my teeth and wait for it to be superseded by next month's "run-it-up-the-flagpole, flavor-of-the-month" chat fad. Unfortunately, it has become more that a temporary verbal tick that eventually dries up of disuse and blows away. It is, in fact, a very bad idea, as in "Yes, chief, we here in the training

Training directors are wasting time and talent trying to prove ROI.

and development unit believe that what we do *must* have demonstrable bottom-line impact, or we shouldn't be doing it."

Now I don't mean to take issue with all those good people who run workshops on how to show that training makes an organizational difference, or who ride the circuit preaching training as a productivity improvement tool. Those, I think, are different issues. But as far as I can see, unless your organization's primary mission is vending training, you aren't entitled to claim that training makes a measurable bottom-line contribution to your organization.

Hold it. Don't go for the rope just yet. My thesis is simple, but wholly reasonable. It goes like this: (A) There are specific people in a for-profit organization who have P&L — bottom line — responsibility. (B) These people are called things like CEO, president, division head, even line manager. (C) All others in a for-profit organization are commonly referred to as support staff. There is a reason for that; it is what they were hired to do — support the men and women who are charged with turning a profit. Their jobs require them to do things like count the coins, watch the legal thicket, make reports, and ensure the people who must produce the products and deliver the services can do just that. All those are good and noble things that need to be done for an organization to survive. But they do not, in and of themselves, generate the dollars and cents, the profit, the "bottom line."

A sales trainer for one of the Big Three auto companies makes the point this way: "We're having a good year. I could go to my boss and attribute XYZ million dollars to my great sales training program. But what if the next year is bad? *How much of the net loss do I claim for my great training programs?* As I see it, you can't have it both ways. If I claim credit for the black ink, I have to accept responsibility for the red. Not likely."

How about the department store trainer who does a whiz-bang job of training Christmas clerks. Does she deserve credit for the store's record season? Or is the marketing person who slashed prices the week before the holiday responsible? Or the ad person who designed the great catalog? How about the store's buyer? Or the economy? How about all of the above?

It is absurd for training or marketing or any staff department to spend time claiming credit for this nickel or that dollar of profit. It takes all of them working together — in service to the front line troops — to make the profit happen. It's called synergy — people working to accomplish together what no one of them could accomplish singly.

Go ahead. Do everything you can to show how useful you are to the corporation. Brag about the courses you've run, the performance problems you've helped solve, the number of great technicians you've sent back to the field. But do yourself a favor. Don't waste your organization's time and your own talent trying to prove impact on the "bottom line." You're too good for that silliness. ■

Don't Change Your Paradigm, Change Your Drill Bit

C all this the paradigm decade. Its roots go back to 1970, when physicist Thomas Kuhn wrote a little book called *The Structure of Scientific Revolutions*. Kuhn argued that the great revolutions in science have been concept-driven. Major breakthroughs result not from solving existing problems but from discovering entirely new ways to think about those problems. He called it paradigm shifting — and launched a revolution in the way we think about innovation and change.

Kuhn's paradigm-shift hypothesis has become influential far beyond the worlds of pure science and academe. Business leaders today are routinely admonished to "shift your paradigm or be left behind," to "learn to see outside the boundaries of conventional perception." There are even paradigm-shifting seminars and training programs:

"Goodbye classroom, hello individualized instruction" is simply the next step in a damnably slow evolutionary march.

Yes, it's true, ladies and gentlemen. In one day you can learn to destroy the old thinking patterns that keep you chained to the past. You'll see yourself, your work, and your world in a whole new light. All this for a mere $199.95.

The wild praise of paradigm shifting as the key to innovation, the pathway to progress, and the final cure for the heartbreak of psoriasis may not be merely excessive but wildly misplaced. That is certainly the view of science historian Freeman Dyson. Writing in an issue of *Physics World*, Dyson contends that scientific revolutions are more often the product of new tools than of new paradigms. They're more likely to result from doing things differently than from thinking about things differently.

"In the last 500 years," writes Dyson, "we have had six major concept-driven revolutions, associated with the names Copernicus, Newton, Darwin, Maxwell, Einstein and Freud. During the same period there have been about 20 tool-driven revolutions." Among the tools of revolution Dyson cites are the telescope and X-ray diffractometer, which wrought dramatic changes in the fields of astronomy and biology.

For those of us in the applied arts and sciences — engineering, business, education, job-skills training — the implication is that focusing on the incremental improvement of the products and processes of our trade is probably a more fruitful and even "progressive" endeavor than, say, sitting under an apple tree waiting for a new paradigm to strike our consciousness.

The problem is, of course, that the paradigm-shift hypothesis makes continuous improvement and incremental change, the stock in trade of tool inventing, seem drab and perhaps even foolish. Who wants to emulate the buggy-whip manufacturer who brought his defect rate down to zero and his cost of product to 15 percent of wholesale price, but missed the advent of the automobile?

The reality of the world around us, however, is that the buggy-whip cases are few and far between. So are the paradigm revolutions.

A 60-Year Overnight Sensation

In the training world, we continue to hear a lot of talk about the imminent demise of classroom training and the meteoric rise of individualized instruction as the replacement "paradigm" of choice. Why? Because of CD-ROM and the computer-based multimedia industry. To an outsider — or a marketer — this may indeed look like a jump shift in thinking. But it is no such thing. The prophesied revolution, if it indeed takes place, will be simply the next step in a very long and damnably slow evolutionary march.

A quick walk through the dusty archives of training-and-development literature will reveal that "Goodbye Classroom, Hello Individualized Instruction" is a theme that has been with us for...well, for quite a while. In a series of articles written between 1926 and 1932, professor Sidney L. Pressey of Ohio State University predicted the "coming industrial revolution in education" and described his invention of "devices that test and teach" students without the intervention of a human teacher.

In one of those articles Pressey lamented that "education is the one major activity in this country which is still in the crude handicraft stage." His complaint has been echoed in the intervening 60-plus years by an illustrious succession of advocates for the teaching machine, programmed instruction, and the multimedia learning cartel.

Meanwhile, all along the way, the B.F. Skinners, the Norm Crowders, the Tom Gilberts, the Geary Rummlers, the Susan Markels, and the Don Bullocks have pushed forward, a step at a time, the basic instructional-design technology that makes individualized instruction actually work. Likewise, CD-ROM, wonderful as it is, is but the latest piece of hardware in a line of inventions that date back to the revolving-drum device that Pressey cobbled together from the guts of a few scrap typewriters, mechanical adding machines and a couple of oak boards.

Don't misunderstand. I'm not denying the potential value of CD-ROM, and I'm certainly not attacking the drive to make widespread individualized instruction a reality. I'm suggesting, rather, that this latest breakthrough, like most important innovations, is more accurately viewed as a product of incremental improvements toward a long-standing goal than as a spectacular leap in perception.

"Invention breeds invention," said Ralph Waldo Emerson. And progress, I suspect, is what happens while we're waiting for our paradigms to shift. ■

Hype Patrol: Is the Multimedia Revolution J.I.T....or R.I.P?

I t's no big secret that I blow hot and cold on multimedia-based training. For years I wrote programmed instruction, developed individualized learning schemes, and pushed and prodded whoever I worked for — or with — to experiment with non-classroom methods. My credo at the time was, "If they can learn it on their own, they should."

The organizational rationale for self-paced multimedia remains clear and compelling. Well-designed computer-delivered instruction can make training: (1) available where and when trainees need it (2) trainee "chunkable" — the learner controls the amount of material and amout of time spent studying it 3) travel-free and 4) interactive media rich.

Missing from automated instruction are those risky exchanges between people who care about ideas.

Over the years, however, the fires of my ardor have been banked by several things. First, there has been experience. By conservative estimate, I've tested and revised and piloted and tinkered with over 100 self-paced products. Some were paper-and-pencil based, some video driven, some computer-based and others in pure multimedia form. And while all eventually met the criterion-level established for them — and a few have even been subjectively rated as "fun" or "interesting" — I have never had a trainee jump up and swear they've just had a life-changing learning experience.

I have, however, seen it more than a few times in a classroom-based seminar. If you buy, as I do, the theory that "affective" influences "cognitive" and "behavioral," that lack is quite troubling.

Sure, the research on individualized instruction shows learning retention is often at or even above classroom-based levels. But lest we forget, learning also takes place through reading, watching TV and walking alone in the woods thinking about life. When you think about it in context, the research on learning retention via multimedia would only be newsworthy if people *didn't* learn from it. Human beings are, if nothing else, highly efficient, natural learning machines, capable of capturing new insights even under the most perverse of conditions. (Or were you never blessed with a college professor who clearly disdained the whole idea of "The Tenured One" being required to address undergraduates, and who lectured with a matching enthusiasm?)

My second cause for pause concerns what happens in a classroom that doesn't happen with CBT or its more evolved cousins. CBT/multimedia can't bond with students, synthesize information, change explanations to respond to unique student inquires, empathize with a student's complaints, problems or points of view, work with large-group dynamics, or quickly adapt to changing student demands. And oh yes, a multimedia program doesn't "feel fulfilled" when a trainee says, "I really enjoyed the day and learned a lot from you." Believe me, training pros miss that kind of feedback — it's one of the things that makes our profession so worthwhile.

Third on my puzzlement list are the listless sales of computer-based and multimedia programs and products. The marketplace, by and large, isn't endorsing the wisdom that the time has come for at-your-desk PC-based training to sweep the world. As far as I can tell from sales charts, even the least-popular computer games are outselling the best educational products by a factor of ten, if not more.

The Answer: Loss of Argumentative Interaction

Ruminating among these observations and my own experiences as a learner leads me to one possible explanation: You can't argue with a computer. You can't take on, fuss with, get mad at or attempt to provoke a computer. It lacks the ability to engage in argumentative interaction.

Some of my most cherished memories of instructional settings in my adult years were those opportunities to passionately engage the instructor, other attendees, and myself at the core. Sometimes the interaction was vicarious, other times personal, strident, and in the spotlight. But in all cases it was engagement with another mind, not an engagement with "content," that was most memorable, and that drew me into an appreciation and passion for the matter at hand. To wit: I, like many I know, was smitten with science by the crystal clear, provocative writing of Issac Asimov. But it wasn't until I was able to sit and talk science with others like myself that I truly caught fire.

Missing from automated instruction are those risky, hot, unpredictable exchanges between people who care about ideas, and who have bruisable egos they willingly put on the line in defense of a point of view. Whether engaged in or simply viewed from afar, it is — if we are honest — these risk-filled moments we remember most vividly as instructor and trainee alike.

Eric Mazur, who teaches an introductory physics course at Harvard University, recently learned the value of that formula. According to an *Associated Press* story, Mazur was distressed when he discovered his students were unable to apply key physics principles to life situations. Mazur dumped his lecture/test approach, gave students his lecture notes, and assigned them discussion questions to present and defend to their classmates. The result: student achievement soared. Mazur's assessment: "It's a matter of engaging the students' brains."

In our zeal to create fail-proof, cost-effective training, have we inadvertently created a boxed formula so unappealing and unchallenging as to rob goal attainment of its real value? I suspect we may well have.

Outsourcing Training: Easier Than You May Be Comfortable Knowing About

Layoffs, once solely the bane of life on the factory floor, have become all too common in the training department as well. The lure of outsourcing is helping to fuel the trend. With field and factory workforces long ago pared to the bone, the only easy economies left to the cost-cutting obsessed are from outsourcing, disbanding, or otherwise doing away with the overhead of in-house staff services. Particularly popular now is outsourcing functions that cannot be justified as key to the direct production of revenues. You name it — accounting, the print shop, payroll, information systems, customer service, and yes, training functions — they are all rapidly being "disowned" and replaced by outside vendors, often at lower costs.

These clues signal that your training group as you know it may soon disappear.

Witness, please, the "in-sourcing" arrangement between Dupont & Co. and the Forum Corp., a Boston-based training consulting firm. Dupont fired most of its in-house training department (some of whom now work for Forum) and handed the keys to the kingdom to Forum. DuPont's motivation was an immediate $8 million reduction in fixed costs, and a 30% reduction in training unit costs. Forum's "win," of course, was a captured client — it is now, in effect, Dupont's training department — and a quantum reduction in its marketing costs.

Somes Clues that You're in the Outsourcing Crosshairs

How do you know if your own training department might be in similar jeopardy? There are a number of obvious and not-so-obvious clues to look for:

1. If questions are routinely raised about your department's costs, if your internal customers are whining more frequently about the hoops you make them jump through to get training, and if your department has been put under a salary and budget freeze, but told to deliver 20% more training for the same bucks and same staff, your operation is probably in the crosshairs. Be doubly alert if someone in senior management starts suggesting that accounting or audit do a "study" to determine "what we're really spending on staff development around here."

2. If your boss's boss has been seen in the executive cafeteria twice in the last fortnight in the company of the president of Acme Training Inc., a $20 million training company with offices on both coasts, start listening for the footsteps. A particularly foreboding indicator: if you are commanded to share your strategic plan with Acme's chief sales honcho.

3. If you start seeing Internet want ads from the same Acme Training Inc. advertising dozens of free-lance or contract training "assignments" in your industry, be advised to start getting chummy with personnel services coordinators in your company's most profitable business units. Emphasize in your discussions the need for those units to have a highly skilled, on-staff training coordinator who can serve as an education "gatekeeper" of sorts, evaluating and running ROIs on all the training the unit will need to continue as the profit standard bearer and growth engine for the corporation.

4. If your boss's boss ends his quarterly report on the health of the company with a little speech using code words and phrases like "focus on core organizational competencies" and "demonstrating clear alignment with organizational outcome goals," head directly to the highest-level supporter of your department and ask for a straight-from-the-shoulder assessment of the theory you are beginning to form. Make it clear you are looking for honesty and advocacy. Make it clear, too, that you are very synergy-minded and want only what is best for the health of the business.

5. If a single vendor is mysteriously and inexplicably retained to do a "comprehensive study of management competencies necessary for success in the coming millennium" and to "recommend a unified development strategy," fast-forward your efforts to update your resume.

Alternately, if you have only a year or two to become vested, suggest that the Acme competency study should really encompass all field and line management responsibilities, as well as overseas subsidiaries. Then volunteer to facilitate the roll-out of that effort. That should ball things up well into the next century. ■

Dumping Human Assets: Corporate America's Quick Fix...and Fatal Error

R obert Krulwich is the resident "simplifier" of ABC News' *Day One* show, a role he previously performed for CBS. Among television newspeople, he seems uniquely skilled at turning technocryptic gobbledygook into monosyllabic English.

On a recent morning news show he incisively explained the rationale behind the current wave of bank and insurance company mergers. He used great props — some paper maché wedding cakes and a box full of plastic people. His method was quaint, quirky, and cute, but his message was not nearly as funny as you might expect. It struck too close to home.

The theory behind the merging of two or more faltering institutions seems to be that if two groups of morons who, for the past decade, have specialized in making irresponsible loans, investing in overpriced commercial real estate, and paying premium prices for marginal acquisitions then merge those mediocre assets — and fire everyone but themselves — synergy will happen and the newly created entity will rise strong and fresh from the rubble of joined incompetencies.

Proving that people are assets worth developing and cherishing remains our biggest challenge.

Whether this increasingly popular gambit will succeed is anyone's guess. After all, the geniuses who thought up this paradigm are the same masterminds who put all those merging megaliths at deep risk in the first place. At the core, however, is a disturbing theorem. As Krulwich put it, "The theory seems to be, 'If we can join enough assets and fire enough people, we should be able to survive.'" Note that people under this theory are an expense to be minimized. People are production units, a curse on the house of organizational existence. Productivity down? Get rid of some people. Get those ratios up. Sales down? Get rid of more people. Get that return on investment up.

More disturbing than the theory itself are the underlying assumptions about the human role in creating capital.

Twenty-five years ago, when I backed into this business, I was fascinated by the idea of employees as assets, and not, as they say in banking, as a "noninterest expense." I was intrigued by the refreshing belief that as people become more experienced and skillful, the more able they are to contribute to solving non-trivial company problems. It seemed an idea well worth championing in the marketplace of ideas.

So what happened? After these many years of you and me and thousands of others like us singing some version of "Invest in people — it pays!" why are we seeing no meaningful trace of our message when organizations are in trou-

ble and making those hard survival decisions?

I'll hazard three possibilities — and a problem:

Theory one: We are wrong. It doesn't work. And those of us in HRD are the only ones who don't get it. The proof? Simple. Only idiots would trash their most valuable resources. Ergo, it didn't work, so we really haven't been having anything close to the organizational impact we believe we've had.

Theory two: The message we've been sending is a self-serving fraud. Knowingly or otherwise, we are simply effecting a placation on Mr. and Ms. Working Stiff. "Yes, you can have a great and rewarding career here at Universal Widgets. And we even have a career development unit staffed by professional caring people ready to help you." We've seduced ourselves. And others. Shame on us.

Theory three: Senior managers do not now nor have they ever believed one milligram of our message. In their view, training's view is just our scam, this "people are developable assets" thing, as surely as "all behavior is marketing behavior" is a marketing department scam for gaining power and budget, and "zero defects drives the market" is the quality assurance pro's scam. It's all interesting — and all minor-point posturing. They learned that in business school.

Which, if any, of these three hypotheses is correct? That's the problem. We don't know, and haven't any way of finding out. Sure, we've all done our bit at showing how this or that new-style training program is an improvement over some older model — or that package "X" gives better back-on-the-job results than package "Y." But that's quite a different — and smaller — matter. Proving the grand claim, and showing its strategic impact in your backyard, that's tougher. Until we can give that sort of evidence, employee development will continue to be like a new coat of paint for the cafeteria — something easily postponed. And employees, like door mats and decaying warehouses, will remain very, very dispensable. ■

Honesty Best Antidote for Rising Workplace Angst

The consensus of the focus group of middle managers I was facilitating was clear, and graphically expressed by one of the bolder participants: "Are you getting the feeling we don't trust top management anymore? Good! Cuz that's the way it is. You play ball with the bosses and you end up with a bat up your nose."

I can't say this is the first time I've had a group of employees tell me they don't trust the management. But the vehemence of the sentiment seems to have taken a quantum leap forward of late. Indeed, the lines between "them" and "us" haven't been so clearly drawn since the labor-management rifts of the 1950s.

The new news is that this is the first time in my experience that the people sitting around the conference room table felt free enough to let it all hang out and openly admit their fears, frustrations, and disappointments.

A sampling of the complaints:

The lines between management and the front lines haven't been so clearly drawn since the 1950s.

■ "When I came into the management trainee program out of college, they said, 'We don't pay newbies as much as some do, but we take care of our own and we pay well in the later years.' Now when the payoff is supposed to be coming my way, they say 'all bets are off.' *After the reengineering here is over, we have to interview for all available jobs. After 20 years, I have to interview for my own job again. The bastards!"*

■ "They don't tell me a thing about whether my operation is valuable, or valued, or even likely to be here next week. They just say cut the costs another 10% and don't hire anyone for the next six months. I don't manage anymore, I just take orders from the golden parachute guys. God only knows where they get their inspiration or what they're really up to."

■ "We make our financial targets and then do what they say. And what they say usually is something like, 'You're doing OK, but you really have to be putting more energy and time into the products of the future — figuring out what will make you successful in the next century.' *Now what the hell does that mean?"*

Trickle-Down Cynicism

What concerns me even more than the low morale among these upper-level middle managers is the impact of their morale on the troops under them.

Back to our focus group — we'll call these middle manager respondents Tom, Dick, and Mary:

Question: *How are your feelings about the company affecting your relations with each other?*

Tom: "The other day someone asked me how I liked the report she did. I said something like, 'You damn people are the neediest bunch I've ever seen. What the hell do you want, gold stars for breathing? Be thankful you've got jobs.'

"For the head of HR, that's pretty bad role modeling. I'm still kissing rears to make up. I even scared me."

Mary: "Hey, for Tom to act like that is really something. He's the one who, in normal circumstances, even gets along with the union guys. I had people telling me about his outburst all day."

Dick: "Cooperation at our level is low. I know I should be as concerned as Tom is about diversity and training and all the HR junk — no offense, Tom — and I should be concerned about Mary's field agents and how the data they get from our system meets their needs. But hey, the company is looking at outsourcing the information technology function anyway, and if some smart outsourcers can convince them that I am superfluous, I'm gone. Or worse, they might keep me to do gopher work and be some kind of 'liaison' between the contractor and us. Some job that will be."

Question: *So, Dick, are you saying you're backing off and taking a wait-and-see approach to the new environment?*

Dick: Wait and see, yeah. But why spend energy on this organization when I know what I do may not count? Why build relations with these guys and then find out our departments aren't even going to be around this time next year? If I'm here and they're not, or they're here and I'm not, it's back to square one either way."

Cost-Cutting Mania Kills Culture

No matter how hard people are working, it often goes for naught unless the organization can bring its cost of doing business into line. But bringing fundamental change runs the risk of killing off the culture that generates and supports the effort needed to make the company successful, regardless of how the organization is reshaped and retooled. And the more rounds of reorganizing, the more debilitating the effect on morale.

Intervening in that downward cycle of change, mistrust, and decaying morale isn't easy. The answer may lie in a simple but powerful tactic: honesty. Leveling with people. Telling them the complete truth of a situation with the belief they can handle whatever is thrown their way. Treating them like adults. Letting them see the future for what it is.

But for most senior managers that is a task beyond their means, better schooled as they are in exuding confidence than in exhibiting candor. In the long run, honesty is much more productive in making change work than is false hope, corny hoopla, or "positive mental thinking" speeches and meetings. ■

Rumble, Rumble: Is That Your Little Training Empire About to Collapse?

Maslow never mentioned it, but I'm convinced empire building is right up there with survival, belongingness, and self-actualization. And it's as big a temptation for training directors as it is for CEOs.

"Empireitis" is an insidious problem — like hypertension, it's hard to detect without skilled professional help. But fear not, like any respectable virus there are some warning signals. If you've noticed two or more of the following in the past 60 days, check with your family career mentor because you may be a prime candidate for a career-crippling crash:

1. You have been toying with the idea of having all walls under your budgetary control painted the same unique color, and all of the file cabinets and metalware electrostatically changed to a distinctive complimentary hue. Chartreuse, perhaps? Your ideal scenario revolves around having the whole thing done over a weekend so you can end that childish dispute with "You-Know-Who" in marketing over exactly whose conference room it is. It's yours, of course.

Power is seductive and can be productive, but in many cases ends up being destructive.

2. You've volunteered to take on the burden of managing the United Way drive, the state Special Olympics meet, the senior management retreat, and the annual stockholders' meeting so that those poor, overworked sweeties in the public relations and corporate communications departments can catch up on their phone calls — and be spared all of those boring trips to Palm Desert. And anyway, all these activities do fit your new department mission statement. (They all involve people.) You will, however, need to double the size of your video department and add three assistants. And seven phone lines. And 18 cubicles. At least.

3. A look at your schedule reveals a surprising number of breakfasts with senior executives lately — at their clubs, at their request, and their treat. A review of post-meeting notes suggests you didn't understand 80 percent of the conversations. The only thing that's clear is that your support was being enlisted for the defense of some project that was somehow of great significance to each. You recall nodding and "tsking" and "umming" and smiling in all of the right places.

4. Your staff training meetings are almost all working lunches, to which you arrive late and leave early, due of course to other, more pressing "corporate level" matters. At each one of these meetings you find you need to single out one of your direct reports to personally "enlighten." Your homily often begins with "I certainly am impressed with the way you have translated theory to practice. However, when I was at Best In The World Corp., I learned that there is a big difference between..."

5. A look at your "to do" list suggests that your most important activity is attending meetings. Staff meetings, breakfast meetings, planning meetings, and then last Wednesday there was the all-day meeting of the task force to investigate excessive meetings. As far as you can tell, there are only two jobs in your organization: going to meetings and answering the phones of people who are in meetings. Today, as opposed to a year or two ago, most of the meetings you go to are meetings you have called. And you now have two people answering your phone while you're in them.

6. Because of all the meetings you go to, you suddenly have acquired an enormous amount of "exciting " new work for your staff. Because of the Compensation Committee meeting, you now have a six-day program on the new performance appraisal system to squeeze into this year's work schedule. As soon as you get the system designed, that is. Because of the Total Quality Committee meeting, you need to send someone from your shop to interview the 11 leading consultants in the field and evaluate them as possible contractors. And the Facilities Beautification Committee — well, you just don't know how to break the news to your staff, but they should understand how this supplemental responsibility will increase the team's value to internal customers. After all, a clean parking lot is a healthy parking lot.

If you recognize yourself, a peer or a boss described by four of these six behavioral anchors, your training empire is in imminent danger of imploding.

The Cure for 'Empire-itis'

But don't panic. As we all know, there is a cure for every social and business disease ever discovered; it's been illegal to invent a problem without a pat solution since 1955. Send a self-addressed, stamped envelope and I'll send you our rates and terms for helping you snuff this pesky bug before you go terminal. I don't want to give away too much information for free, but I will tell you we employ a case study methodology. Among my favorite cases are Big Julie Caesar, and, everybody's current favorite, Saddam Maddman. ■

Trend Toward 'Incredibly Shrinking Training Modules' Has a Dark Side

The client meeting had been clearly labeled and advertised well in advance: *The Absolutely Final, Speak Your Mind Or Forever Hold Your Peace Client Survey Review Meeting.* So it was a little disconcerting when two of the attendees asked, "Like, so what's this meeting all about?" before the decaf had even stopped swirling in the cups. Hoping the comments were simply a pair of lame attempts at humor, I plowed on, introducing the agenda and starting review. But within a few seconds, it became obvious that the only participant who had been through the review material was the customer affairs director for the client company, the person who had first commissioned the work.

To say she wasn't terribly happy with her peers — her internal clients, actually — would be a huge understatement. And to say that her Critical Parent rose to the surface would be very accurate, and in retrospect a wonder to behold: *"What the bloody @$!*#*! are we doing spending all this time creating custom-designed surveys if you aren't interested enough to give us some little inkling of what you want to know about your customers?"* she asked in her most scalding tone.

Silence.

"If this is all the enthusiasm we can muster for getting the right questions down, what's going to happen when the data starts coming back and there are weekly reports to deal with?"

More silence.

Finally a senior vice president cleared his throat and spoke up. "Sherrie, you're absolutely correct, in theory. But there isn't a person here including yourself who doesn't have a briefcase full of memos, reports, and a backlog of e-mail to deal with every night. We all were banking on everyone else digging into this one, that's all. Of course this project is important to us, but it's just one of 20 projects that are of vital interest to everyone in this room. You toss a coin and hope those projects you spend your time on are the right ones for the company, and that you don't get caught without your homework done too often."

Training on the Run

I remember that meeting and the SVP's self-effacing confession so vividly not only for the refreshing candor, but for his use of the word *homework*. More and more we are hearing reports of managers routinely putting in a minimum of three to six hours weekly at home on top of the now "normal" 50-hour work week. Front-line employees are no less pressed for optional time.

The fallout for training departments is that it's becoming harder and harder to find time — either during or after work hours — when employees can

attend training sessions. And when the time is found, the howling over anything longer than half-day programs can be deafening. In defense, many training executives have been actively searching for creative delivery alternatives, which is a polite way of saying you're learning the art of how to sandwich and shoehorn training time around other activities.

In healthcare, trainers have been forced into using around-the-clock, 45-minute pre- and post-shift training "packagettes" supplemented by trainer-facilitated roundtable discussions in coffee rooms and break areas. In the retail, hospitality, and fast food industries, structured OJT has been dusted off and brought back to life. There are myriad other examples of "The One-Minute Trainer." Call it training on the run.

Treating Training As an Equal

But central to all these efforts to mold training around the reality of long hours and thinned ranks is the tacit assumption that employees can and will pick up the training slack in their free time, off hours. In the jargon of the day, professional development is becoming self development. The dark side of that proposition is the assumption that employees' lives are somehow less hectic and jam packed off the job than on. That's a dubious presumption, at best.

Ultimately, this demand dilemma can only be satisfactorily resolved by a rethinking of the value of training relative to other organizational improvement efforts. If training is to be a key part of an organization's value system and culture, it has to be planned for, budgeted for, and treated as an equal to any other important part of employees' work lives. It can't be treated as an afterthought, necessary evil, or nuisance to be taken care of between meetings or during bathroom breaks. ■

In Defense of Fad Surfing

At the Training Directors' Forum Conference in Phoenix this spring, the ever-incisive Peter Drucker perched casually on the edge of a table in a spacious meeting room and told some 350 corporate training managers that "five years from now, nobody will be talking about teams." All of the continuing furor about team-building and self-managing work teams amounted to much ado about nothing — faddish at best, counterproductive at worst. So declared the most venerable management thinker in the world.

The gathered were by turns amused and apoplectic ("My gosh! He's not kidding. He means it!"), which only goaded Herr Professor to elaborate. For starters, Drucker said, "You all think there is one kind of thing called a team." Wrong. The dynamics of a baseball team are wildly different from those of a soccer team. The dynamics of a symphony orchestra are wildly different from those of a string quartet or a jazz combo. The same is true in offices and factories among groups with different tasks and missions. When you teach "teamwork" as if it means substantially the same thing for everyone in every job, you're teaching nonsense. And you destroy any value that the basic concept might have offered.

The secret is not to eschew fad following, but to use it to your advantage.

As for self-managing teams, Drucker continued, they presuppose that *everyone* will exercise excellent judgment all of the time. "How much great judgment have you seen in your life?" he asked dryly. Even companies that have used work teams for decades still find them frustrating. Two years ago, Drucker asked Toyota's head of manufacturing how his teams were doing. The answer: "We've got one that works and 11 that don't."

Drucker challenged his doubters to ask two questions: What results have we achieved with teams? And over what period of time? Then the nonbelievers should go find some workers who have been trained as "team players" and ask a third question: "What are you being paid for?" The answers to these lines of inquiry, he warned, would not be encouraging.

Ah! Another Emperor busted for indecent overexposure. Another in the endless sea of glitzy management fads called to its day of reckoning.

Fad Surfing. That's what management consultant Eileen Shapiro calls it: "the practice of riding the crest of the latest management panacea and then paddling out again just in time to ride the next one; always lucrative for consultants and absorbing for managers, frequently disastrous for the organization." In *Fad Surfing in the Boardroom: Reclaiming the Courage to Manage in the Age of Instant Answers* (Addison-Wesley, 1995), Shapiro recounts the pitfalls associated with blindly following the bright lights of the latest Great Management Idea. And she's right.

The Glow and the Tingle

But there is also a positive side to the impulse to toss off the old and take on the new, to try something, anything — this thing — to refresh interest and revive effort in an organization. Call it halo, call it placebo, call it Hawthorne effect, call it what you like, but an undeniable energy infuses the urge in the business world today to break, change and tinker with things.

Yes, we can and do rationalize it all with fabulous hypothetical numbers and computations. And yes, we do solemnly swear to evaluate as we go along and to pull the plug the minute the panacea appears to be pooping out. But any promoter worth his salt can gin up a regression analysis or factor-weighted scoring scheme to "prove" the efficacy of the idea he's hawking. The fact is, plugs are never pulled because of questionable results — only on account of yawns.

Where the rubber really hits the road is in what Paul Sherlock, author of *Rethinking Business-to-Business Marketing* (Free Press, 1991), calls "the glow and tingle" of the idea: "You're sitting across the table from a would-be customer. You lovingly describe your new gee-whiz gizmo. At some point you see the prospect's eyes light up. You've got him."

Regardless of what you read, business runs on ideas, not on the bottom line. And in the marketplace of ideas, glow and tingle are hugely important. Glow and tingle attract both prince and peasant. Glow and tingle keep the tinkerers tinkering until the widgets finally work and prove their mettle. Glow and tingle lure us out of bed and onto the freeway on days when rationality would dictate sleeping in, feigning a disease, and fishing from the end of a dock.

Run 'Fads' Through This 5-Question Screen

The secret is not to eschew fad following, but to use it to advantage. I like to sift new fancies through a screen five questions deep:

(1) Is it easy to understand the outcomes that are being promised?

(2) Are those outcomes obviously important to the organization?

(3) Must you suspend your belief in the laws of nature in order to see the connection between the experience prescribed and the outcome promised?

(4) Will failure of the idea to bear fruit harm the organization or anyone in it (save the idea's champion)?

(5) Will the idea create a glow that excites people and focuses them, at least for a while, on some meaning beyond the next paycheck?

Two "yes's," two "no's" and an "absolutely" are enough for me to give the green light. To paraphrase my second-cousin Jolly, "If it ain't illegal, immoral or fattening, and it's any fun at all, it's probably worth doing." ∎

Second Chances: Dreamers See Training Space As a Place for New Hope

The ubiquitous holiday party. Small talk. Idle chatter. Stock questions and superficial answers. I toss at an acquaintance this no brainer: "Seen any of the new holiday movies?" The chap leans toward my ear, drops his party smile, and lowers his voice to a conspiratorial whisper. His eyes dart from side to side to be sure we aren't being overheard by Smith Barney, the KGB, or our respective spouses.

"*Hook!*" he exhales through lips barely parted, while pressing his right forefinger across the center of his mouth.

"*Hook?*" I respond, in an incredulous tone. "*Really?*"

He shushes me with both hands, reinspects the room and, apparently convinced the confidentiality of our conversation has not been breached, hisses an explanation: "Really! It's not for kids at all. It speaks to you. Quite poignant. Makes you think about relationships and parenting and the kid inside and doing something exciting with your life. Know what I mean?"

The economy calls for lean and mean, but the spirit of the times calls for stirring childish hopefulness.

I certainly did — or at least I thought I had a pretty good idea of what he was getting at. This was, you see, the same graying grown-up who only a fortnight before had given me an impassioned endorsement of the Billy Crystal movie *City Slickers*, and had waxed on about his feeling that no one — no "guy" that is — over 35 could fail to see some sense of his own frustrations and lost direction in the characters played by Crystal and his band of corporate ciphers.

Beyond a Seasonal Trend

But wait a minute — don't we all get a little misty-eyed, nostalgic and, well, just plain dopey at Christmas? What with Yule logs, caroling and 24-hour-a-day screenings of *It's a Wonderful Life?* It's awfully hard not to be caught up in the spirit of the day and remembrances of times past. Of course we're all rendered more emotional. We know it's going to happen, and we look forward to it.

But there is, I think, a trend beyond this predictable seasonal happening. I suggest that a disproportionate number of us are getting caught up in a nostalgia for roads not taken and adventures not lived — and a search for, at the very least, symbolic recompense and second chances.

It fits the generation mellowing into middle age spread to a fair-thee-well, doesn't it? The generation of JFK, *Hair*, Vietnam, and the Beatles that saw the world as a place ripe for reworking at their hands. And who are just now discovering that they didn't really pull it off.

And it also works for those just one generation behind: the Yupsters and the generation of Alex Keaton look-alikes and Ivan Boesky wanna-be's weaned on stock quotes and leveraged buyouts, who have seen their heroes revealed for what they are. A generation heavy into rethinking itself and at the very extreme looking for a personal answer to the Peggy Lee question: "Is this all there is to life?"

Nostalgia as Training Content

And as surely as art mirrors life, this nostalgia for the what-might-have-beens has stomped its way into your training spaces. How else do you account for the rush to African safari team-building experiences, to "white-water canoeing for improved profits" adventures, and to the "swinging from ropes for job enrichment" courses that are so popular today? Or for the Robert Bly inspired "Discovering Your Warrior Self" seminars? Or the fascination with Joseph Campbell's "myths and heroes" writings and theories?

Child psychiatrist Bruno Bettelheim, like Campbell, believed that we all experience our lives in some way through the myths and fairy tales we carry along with us from childhood to adult life. Of the adult fairy tale, he wrote, "they satisfy childhood wishes which remain unfulfilled, and which in most of us remain unacknowledged, and they do so in ways that were not available to the child, in ways that can be satisfied only by adults."

We've been busy telling each other that training in the '90s will have to be leaner, meaner, less conceptual, more practical and pragmatic, more bottom-line justified. Probably all true prescriptions. But incomplete. If I read my friend and the marketplace trends right, training into the 21st Century is also going to have to find ways to challenge and ignite the child and the childish, the hopefulness and the visions, and perhaps most of all, the mythical hero in us all if we are to be truly focused and fired for the challenges ahead. ■

Managers: They Have Enough to Do Without Making Them Be Trainers, Too

Every couple of years someone rediscovers the simple fact that supervisors and front-line managers have a lot of influence on the way front-line employees do their jobs, a revelation that invariably leads to the conclusion that first-line supervisors and managers are ducky candidates for jobs as part-time trainers.

That sounds good, but I think that in most cases "manager as trainer" is a fantasy.

Sure, in some circumstances manager as trainer is the most practical solution to the problem of training employees with minimum cost and delay. It's true, too, that this method is probably the oldest and still the most frequently exercised way of training employees, especially employees newly hired for minimum- and modest-skills jobs, and for new employee orientation. But, at the very least, this quaint idea discounts managerial work as work and views front-line work simplistically.

Asking line managers to train discounts managerial work as 'real' work.

Managing and supervising *is* work. I think it was Peter Drucker who first suggested that management should not be considered something a person does in addition to his or her real work, but a form of real work itself. A friend of mine with a training staff of 20 told me recently she almost came unglued the day her boss, in an offhanded manner, suggested that "Once you get this department shaped up, you'll be able to get back to the classroom 80 or 90 percent of the time, won't you?"

Made her wonder just what he thought they were teaching in their management courses.

But turn that around. How do you think the average line manager or first-line supervisor — the survivors of your organization's last downsizing — would react to the news that not only are they picking up a raft of new people to manage, but the responsibility for training them — by hand — too?

It also strikes me as a severe discount to trainers and the training process to cavalierly suggest that any competent manager should be able to pinch hit. Some can, but they are the exceptions. One of the best lending officers I ever met, a fellow who could actually make me not only understand, but enjoy the subject of lending— a guy who is creative, responsive and a prince among paupers one-on-one with the most cantankerous of corporate CEOs — is a stick in front of a group.

As a Q&A expert visiting with trainees who had mastered the basics, he was great, but he couldn't lead a silent prayer.

Subject Matter Expertise

Asking managers to act as trainers assumes that they have, or can easily acquire, the knowledge necessary to enlighten the troops. Two problems: First, many of the training programs organizations use, such as those to improve quality, service and productivity, have content with which a manager or first-line supervisor is as likely to be unfamiliar as anyone else in a work group. While it might at first seem reasonable to equip the manager to handle that material, it most frequently is not. This is especially true of the mundane but important day-to-day kind of training most training professionals get involved with that managers should not.

Take a "simple" program such as employment interviewing, for instance. Training companies like DDI and Drake Beam Morin place a lot of emphasis on the training they provide people who will train others to do interviewing. The legal liability under which a sloppy interview can place an organization is such that these companies want to be darned certain they aren't exposed. Multiply the days and dollars it would take to train all the managers in your organization to train their people in risk-free interviewing, and the idea of using managers in this fashion is plainly ludicrous.

Even with the best pre-programmed, automated, and scripted packaged program, a line manger is a poor substitute for a yeoman trainer who is skilled at handling groups.

There are organizations that ignore this prejudice of mine, some for good reasons. Take as an example the approach Xerox Corp. used to introduce employee participation and quality improvement. As part of the company's *Leadership Through Quality* program, every manager went through training twice, once as a member of a management group and once as a leader of a "family group" — the group he or she supervised. But there is quite a difference in my mind between day-to-day training activities and this massive culture change effort involving 100,000 employees.

As organizations downsize and automate, managers themselves become less competent in the specifics of the jobs they supervise. Managers have to come to grips with management by influence rather than by superior knowledge and intimidation. They are going to have to rely on the professionals who work for them — their direct reports and the staff training people — to keep the expertise of their crack troops at state-of-the-art ready.

Maybe I'm selling managers and supervisors short; perhaps they're just dying to take training under their wings, to do personally and by hand what they now assign to others. Maybe, but I really doubt it. ■

Diversity Training
As Punishment

The continuing unfolding of the lurid saga of Cincinnati Reds owner Marge Schott has proven strangely instructive. Her case has served not only as a lightning rod for champions of many diverse causes, but as a spooky commentary on the cause called diversity.

Schott's troubles began when she was sued by a former controller of her baseball team over his dismissal. Schott countersued, and the whole thing ended up in a very public trial. Sworn statements from former employees accused Schott of egregious racial insensitivity. Specifically, she is said to have referred to designated hitter Dave Parker and outfielder Eric Davis as "my million-dollar niggers." Other non-Anglo-Saxon employees fared no better. Schott reportedly was "perplexed," for instance, upon learning that Tim Sabo, the ex-controller, was offended by one of her little hobbies: collecting Nazi memorabilia. Sabo is Jewish.

Diversity training has become the cultural counterpart to traffic school.

As these and other allegations surfaced, more sensibilities were offended, tempers flared and the fun began. Henry Aaron, Jessie Jackson, the Jewish Anti-Defamation League, Rush Limbaugh and any number of special-interest groups waded into the fray.

A spokesperson for a feminist group said in *USA Today* that Schott was being persecuted because of her gender. Civil libertarians fretted about the threat posed by political correctness to the spirit of the First Amendment. "Whatever happened," asked one, "to 'I do not agree with what you say, but will defend to the death your right to say it'?" A prominent therapist who works with recovering alcoholics allowed that if, as alleged, Schott is overly fond of John Barleycorn, she shouldn't be held accountable for much of anything anyway.

In what was widely regarded as an epic feat of hypocrisy, the executive council of the Major League Baseball Association (MLBA) launched an investigation of Schott's moral fitness to own a baseball team. The council settled upon her punishment: a $25,000 fine, a one-year suspension from baseball and enrollment in an approved program of diversity training.

That last part bears repeating. As retribution for her sins, Schott is sentenced to a term of diversity training: "Madam, for the crime of attitudinal reprehensibility, you are remanded forthwith to the custody of the nearest sensitivity adjuster. Next case."

The MLBA was far from original in conceiving diversity training as a form of punishment. Over the past few years, courts have imposed the same penalty on managers and employees of any number of organizations that have lost or settled legal cases involving racial discrimination or sexual harassment. Schott's case is, however, the most notorious illustration to date of the concept of diversity training as a sort of cultural counterpart to traffic school.

Ever been to traffic school? It's a favorite recourse of judges in a number of states. After about your third moving violation, your driver's license is suspended until you've given up five evenings to footage of gory highway fatalities, badly made public-service videos, and badly delivered lectures on defensive driving and the evils of mixing alcohol with gasoline. Class dismissed.

Years ago I helped revise a traffic-school curriculum for a national association. During this stint I spent some time in Dade County, FL, conducting focus groups with offenders sentenced to traffic school. Talk about diversity! This was Noah's Ark. Snowbirds, punks, truck drivers, hookers, high schoolers, Cuban fishermen, speed freaks, several Laotians who spoke not a word of English, a minister, a rabbi, a little old lady from New Jersey, plus — I'm not making this up — a biker named T-Rex, who wore a chicken bone through his nose, and his girlfriend, Roxie.

A Classic 'Spray & Pray'

Learnings gleaned from group interviews with this sample of vehicular desperadoes: (a) They all knew they were breaking the law when they broke it. (b) They all knew how not to break the law. (c) They all intended to be smarter in the future about not getting caught breaking the law. Some of them, it's true, would accomplish this by breaking the law less often. But nobody ever emerged from traffic school with what honestly might be called a heightened sense of "appreciation" or "valuing" or "respect" for the traffic regulations (or the traffic-school instructors) of Dade County, FL.

I suspect that Marge Schott will be similarly affected by her diversity-school experience.

Will she then be more "sensitive" to minority employees? Maybe in the same sense that speeders are sensitive to the possibility of radar traps. Will she be more likely to hire and promote minorities into the front-office management of her ball club? Probably not. Will she in any sense have "learned her lesson"? Only if the lesson is to keep a closer guard on her tongue, and to walk among people who are "different" in much the same way she might walk among clumps of poison ivy.

What about the rest of us? What will we learn from the Schott affair? That valuing diversity is about using the right words? That when accused of using the wrong words, the best course of action is to grovel, sing a chorus of "We Are the World," and remember to hire good lawyers? That diversity training is about doing your time and learning not to get caught again? I wonder. ■

Multiculturalism: Is the Focus on Appreciation and Respect...or Revenge?

I used to think I knew what the term multiculturalism meant and what the diversity training movement was all about. I thought multiculturalism was about the simple fact that we — all of us — live in an increasingly heterogeneous society and work in increasingly heterogeneous organizations.

The diversity dialogue, I was led to believe, was about the fact that organizations that stop short of striving for a fully integrated, harmoniously functioning workforce will be big losers in the scramble for talent and customers at home and abroad. Diversity training, I thought, was an effort to acquaint managers, supervisors and executives of the facts of multiculturalism and the legal, moral, and productive ramifications of ignoring the changing nature of who shows up for work when the shift whistle blows.

Diversity training, I thought, was about creating awareness and changing some overt behavior; awareness that people of all identifiable racial, ethnic, religious, circumstantial, and nationality groupings have a sense of person and pride about their specific uniqueness and differences.

Characteristically, this training was to be offered to all, but primarily aimed at heterosexual white males under the assumptions that (a) most in the managerial ranks are heterosexual white males and (b) that some heterosexual white males have, in the past, carried out their responsibilities in ways that are indifferent, insensitive, or somehow painful to the sensitivities of employees not like themselves in age, race, religion, national origin, and/or situation. The core messages of those programs, I was led to believe, was about legalities, logistics, and some simple humanitarian values. Among those values: Tolerance is good, bigotry is bad; working harmoniously is better than working under conditions of intimidation and coercion; and no race, culture, or religion is "better" or produces more "worthy" people than any others.

Diversity training too often seems about getting even, not getting along.

An Altered View

But lately, I've begun to think my understanding of the multicultural movement has been extremely "Boy Scout" and naive.

In far too many instances, I am learning, the multicultural movement seems to be about getting even and turning the tables; about reversing the roles of insulted and insulted — with impunity. How else would you explain a recent review of the opening of A.R. Gurney's "Love Letters" at a Minneapolis dinner theater that begins with:

"Nothing could sound more boring than listening to two actors read WASP love letters aloud on stage."

What other rationale can there be for a running Nickelodeon gag ad for a boxed breakfast food called "Whities" that tells young viewers:

"Two helpings and you dance geeky, smile stupidly, shake hands like a dweeb, and play golf."

Innocent fun? I don't think so.

In far too many corporate classrooms the agenda, while more subtle, is equally clear: The instruction of non-minority group members — primarily white males — about the sins of their forefathers toward "people of difference," the role of "their kind" in the oppression and humiliation of people of difference, and the importance of these trainees accepting their personal responsibility in the perpetuation of the same said sins.

Suspect, do you, that I've a case of Limbaugh-noia? Possible, but consider the experience of Andrew Ferguson, a senior writer for the magazine *The Washingtonian*, who reported on his experiences at the National Multi-Cultural Institute's "Building Personal and Professional Competence in a MultiCultural Society" conference in a recent issue of his magazine.

During a train-the-trainer workshop Ferguson attended, he was told:

■ The purpose of diversity training is "not just about understanding, it's *about changing who you are.*"

■ The roots of inequity are the power-hunger and arrogance of white-male ethnocentrism and their offspring — capitalism. "Sharing power is not something a male-dominated culture naturally gravitates toward," he was told. "We must create a setting where the powerful want to make changes toward the multicultural. Sometimes force is necessary. If more won't do this on their own, then a force situation will become necessary."

■ And finally, he was told the ultimate goal of diversity training is to induce personal epiphanies in the form of such statements as, "I am a recovering sexist," and, "I accept the 'onion theory' that I will continue to peel away layers of my own racism for the rest of my life."

In my naiveté, I still believe diversity training ought to be about equality and fairness, appreciation, and reciprocal respect. But to a growing cadre of advocates it seems diversity is simply about power, who has it, who hasn't, and how one group can wrest it from another. It is hardly a new or enlightened idea. It is simply yet another scarcity driven, zero-sum idea whose time has come — and will go —and is destined to leave behind yet another helping of disappointment, frustration, and doubt. ■

A Year of Living Differently Gives New Meaning to 'Acceptance'

Four years ago, I joined the ranks of the "handicapped." OK, so I didn't exactly join in the "volunteered for duty" sense of the word. I was drafted. I lost a vocal cord.

OK, I didn't exactly lose it in the "where the hell are my car keys" sense. Nor did I euphemistically lose it in the sense it was chopped out and tossed in the dead organs pail either. It's in the same place it's been the last 50-plus years, it just doesn't work anymore.

The plan is for a clever surgical Pooh-Bah to implant something that looks like the butt end of a plastic spoon in this wayward cord. If all goes well, I will, with practice, be able to approximate a normal human speaking voice — or a very expensive duck call.

I won't be back screaming at ball games anytime soon, but if all goes as promised (I do believe, Peter, I do believe!) I will no longer have to spend my time at social gatherings smiling and nodding while the "normal" people around me hold actual conversations. Whatever the outcome, my perspective has changed on the relationship between the fully functioning, able-bodied world to — dare I say it — "the handicapped." A single year of personal experience and introspection is hardly a basis for a great manifesto about being handicapped, but I have a few observations that seem worth sharing.

All of us are just trying to get by with a little style and dignity. For some of us that's a little harder than for others.

1. Disabled and handicapped people make us uncomfortable — if not plainly fearful.

We see our own mortality and potential for fragility in the obviously handicapped, and it scares us. We don't know how we would react to a loss of the same capacity as that staring us in the face — and we'd rather not have to think about it.

I had encountered this phenomenon in regard to people with severe limitations before: "Oh come now, you don't really expect us to let one of *them* wait on our customers do you?" But I was still taken aback when it first happened to me because of my diminished voice. Twice I've had meeting planners explain to me they couldn't possibly put me in front of their group: "It would be just too distracting and uncomfortable for them." One went so far as to explain: "I need the meeting to end on an up note and well...you understand." What made these encounters especially memorable was that one of the people was planning a meeting for a fast-food company that brags about its "diverse hiring" practices. The other was planning for a large healthcare group.

2. We often confuse disability with sickness.

Some disabled people are ill. Most are not. Most are about as prone to the vagaries of colds, the flu, upset stomach, hangovers, bad days, and the blahs as any of us. And they are as prone to having good days, good ideas, highs, the giggles, and fun times as well.

I'd like a dollar for every flight attendant who has offered me hot tea with lemon and honey and whispered, "Do weeb hab a cold?" after I've done my Godfather-ish, "Good morning."

3. We expect the handicapped to be "Super Crips" at work.

At the opposite extreme from the illness assumption is the assumption that anybody who comes to work in a wheelchair, or using sticks, or is unsighted is one driven, high-powered son (or daughter) of a gun. The fact is that the disabled are no more and no less career-minded or achievement-driven than anyone else. They do what they do for the same reasons we all do: because they want to, because they have to, and because they need to.

I vividly remember the startled looks and terse mutterings engendered by an old acquaintance, a wheelchair-bound consultant, who tended to call it out when people acted dumb on elevators — as in not making room for him to wheel out at his floor — and when he made hard remarks about seminar rooms set up badly for handicapped presenters. His quick temper, harsh remarks, and total lack of forbearance fit neither the Super Crip nor the Helpless Harry images. *He was simply human.*

Perhaps what I've learned in my year of living differently is this: All of us — abled, disabled, tall, short, black, white, brown, yellow or green — are simply trying to get by with a little style, a little dignity, and a little grace. That's a little harder for some than others, but it's never a cake walk. The biggest differences between "them" and "us" are those we create in our own minds. And the acceptance of those different from ourselves is nothing more and nothing less than the acceptance of ourselves. ■

Take It Personal: Mitsubishi Sexual Harassment Case Is Black Eye for HRD Profession

We lean toward tenderness in the training trade. We put a lot of faith in the basic goodness of our fellow humans. We like to think that through reason, understanding, and compassion we can change attitudes and opinions — and move the world. Sometimes it works. Often it doesn't, at least not where attitudes are entrenched and perverse behavior is self-reinforcing.

Case in point: The alleged rampant sexual harassment of female workers at the Mitsubishi Motors plant in Normal, IL. So far, some 300 women have voiced complaints to the EEOC against the automobile manufacturer, the largest sexual harassment suit in history. They allege that Mitsubishi management for years looked the other way while a fusillade of assaults and affronts took place. Name calling, butt pinching, breast groping, and a prostitute hired for a company picnic are but some of the charges. Getting the picture? We're not talking about over-extended eye contact or the murmuring

Where were HR and training while this tragic situation was building?

of politically incorrect appellations or "general discomfort" with the tone of the working environment. We're talking assault, threats, and overt hostility toward women in the workplace.

The company's reaction? Why, Mitsubishi management apparently loaded up some buses with local bubbas and barbies and drove to Chicago and picketed the regional EEOC office.

Geez, that tactic worked for Hooters, didn't it?

Do you start to get the feeling the collective genealogy of this fine management team could make that kid on the porch in the movie *Deliverance* look a little like a direct descendent of Albert Einstein?

Where Was Voice of HRD?

Two questions: (1)Where were our HR and training brethren while this tragic situation was building? (2) Would you care to hazard a guess what punishment the courts will mete out to this motley crew when this case finally gets to court?

Last question first. If you answered "sensitivity training" as punishment, you win the cookie. Training? These lads need caning worse than they need training. Well, OK, maybe training in the form of a whack across the bridge of the nose with a rolled-up *Fortune* magazine every time one of them starts drooling on his shoes. But training in the "let's sit down and discuss proper workplace behavior among adult men and women in 1996" sense? I don't think so. Maybe, just maybe, if these dimwits instead were sentenced to walk backwards in high heels from Normal, IL, to Chicago with a gang of besotted tugboat captains pinching their ears with electrical pliers, they might get the hint and begin to see things as those harassed women employees were forced to. But I wouldn't wager a week's salary on it.

Instead, how about a very public "Stop that!" followed by a firm, *"You're fired."*

Unless someone has repealed the proven laws of behavior, the direct viewing of dire consequences greatly decreases the likelihood that the observed behavior will be incorporated into the viewer's repertoire.

But question number one is the real conundrum for me. Where were the HR— and HRD — folks who supposedly minister to the tribes of that little plant on the prairie? I can think of only three reasons the folks from our fraternity didn't blow the big fire siren on the water tower in the Normal town square. They are, in ascending order of contemptibility: (1) Approval. (2) Complicity. (3) Cowardice.

We talk a great game, many of us, about influencing people and events beyond the mere scope of the workplace. We like to think, some of us, that we do deeds of great social consequence. And we mewl mightily about the lack of respect we receive for all of our good works. Perhaps, just perhaps, the respect we crave requires us to do a bit more than just come to work, do well, stay out of trouble, and live long. Perhaps the respect we seem to crave so much needs a few courageous acts and a little valor behind it. Acts like standing up and calling it out when something just plain wrong is going on — and there must have been plenty of early warning signs — regardless of how unpopular that vertical rise may be. Acts like saying "Stop!" even when those around you aren't in the mood for truth-telling and won't love you instantly for saying it. Acts like "doing the right thing" exactly when nobody will respect you for it...except, of course, for yourself.

Journalist Jimmy Breslin once said, "Power is funny. Whether you think you have it, or whether you think you don't — you're right."

Respect, perhaps, is like that as well. It starts on the inside, or it doesn't start at all. ■

Guys, We Gotta Play a Major Role in Solving Sexual Harassment Problem

Guys, we as a gender group have been getting some bad press lately. Bad unless you happen to be one of the cretins who can't see a woman without leering, lurching, or slobbering on your shoes.

The problem, as I see it, is that we've been asking for this. Really, we have. Personal behavior aside — and who among us could feel comfortable running for public office in the current climate? — we've all been guilty of benign neglect. Who among us has not simply turned his head when some dufus, some powerful senior dufus, has made one of those hoary "secretary as office equipment" jokes? And we've been pretty much missing-in-action on the intervention front as well. Do you know many guys who've been willing to facilitate a "Sexual Harassment and You" program? No, me neither. We've acted like sexual harassment is a "for women only" issue and stayed out of the way so as not to be in danger of being identified with it.

The result has been the development of some interventions that, frankly, seem to me to address sexual harassment all wrong. If the problem is by and large a "guy thing" then so too must be the solution. No, I'm not going to suggest that a better intervention would be one of those Robert Bly, eat-raw-rabbit-and-pound-on-drums things. But I am suggesting that a better intervention might be guys facing guys and getting some things straight, without a female audience.

The first challenge is to change behaviors — and then hope that changes in attitude will follow.

Look, if you've read *You Don't Understand*, by Deborah Tanner — or one of the more recent clones — and you get the point that a frequent result of women and men attempting to communicate is that they miscommunicate, then you know where I think we need to be that we aren't. It strikes me that the solution to sexual harassment has to be as much a guy thing as is the problem. That means no hiding behind sexually neutral or neutered corporate-speak and mixed-group politeness. Here's my approach:

(1) Treat sexual harassment as a compliance problem, not a religious conversion or political correctness problem. There are guidelines for conduct. Follow them to the letter and the spirit and everything's fine. This *is not* a freedom of speech or testosterone issue.

(2) Make a 15-minute video. This would feature women in a focus group reacting to the lines guys use in the workplace to prove to themselves and their buddies that women enjoy guys constantly carrying on like moose in rutting season...*not*. That should bend a few egos and put a couple of myths to bed — alone.

(3) For the incorrigibles — those Clarence Thomas judiciary committee members who couldn't seem to "get it" and other borderline dull subnormals — there should be an advanced session called "Sexual Harassment: The Personal Consequences." Topics to be covered:

• The law, corporate policy and 10 things that will get you fired in less time than it takes to clean out your locker and turn in your pass. Include names of those who didn't believe this part of the program and their dates of involuntary termination.

• Rules for "hunting chicks" in the workplace. *Rule One:* Forget it. *Rule Two:* When in doubt, reread Rule One.

• An optional segment, for the tediously socially handicapped, might cover male-female personal communication in non-power related situations outside the workplace (subtitled: "How to Talk With Women Who Aren't Being Paid To Listen") and how to ask out a co-worker without feeling like a kid at a junior high sock hop, or coming off like a potential pervert.

(4) Develop a process, called "Calling Out the Cretins," for those who despite policies and training, still need a couple of quick jerks on the choke chain to get the point. A process that is straight, direct, usable by average working Joes and "guy" friendly. That is, guys will call out the malefactors but it won't result in a loss of a down or a rotation on the bowling team.

The deal is, guys, we've been standing around with our hands in our pockets looking at our shoes long enough. If you believe it's time to put an end to sexual harassment, do something. If you don't like my approach, do something else. But do something. Face it down, get it over and done with. Get it off the agenda. There's no way we can be effective attacking the productivity and quality problems in our companies if half of "we" is being distracted by this pointless perversion of male-female relations. ∎

There's No Such Thing As a 'Safe' Training Zone

To the seasoned trainer, the training room can feel like a safe haven, a shelter from the storms of real life. But for the nonprofessional trainee, and that includes most of them, the training room is a place of high emotion, significant consequences, and very much a part of the real world.

That came to mind the other morning while reading a forthright "Manager's Journal" column in *The Wall Street Journal* by Debra Benton, a Fort Collins, CO, training consultant.

Long and short: Benton was accused of sexual harassment as a result of teaching a sexual harassment seminar. Her transgression was to touch the bare knee of a Bermuda-shorts-clad male participant — in plain view of 50 other participants — as a demonstration of inappropriate touch in the workplace. The touchee and his spouse, who was not an attendee, complained to his employer that they felt sexually harassed and demanded the company cease using Benton as a vendor. Though she was, in her words, "cleared of any wrongdoing," the hubbub cost her what had started out to be a seven-year engagement.

> *A trainer's view of safe harbor can be a trainee's picture of a dangerous port of call.*

The story caused me pause because I think most of us are prone to making up these spur-of-the-moment demonstrations during seminars. Similar to Benton's unfortunate gaff, I once draped myself over the wrong lady's shoulder to demonstrate behavior a service rep should feel free to rebuff. Fortunately for me her black belt was in bad mouth and not martial arts. The beating cured me of touching without prior permission.

But at the heart of this problem are three faulty assumptions about training rooms being safe havens for trainees.

Dumb Assumption #1: *Training is a no-pressure respite from the work-a-day world.*

The square-one assumption of all training is that people learn better and faster if they are away from the job, focused on a specific set of ideas and performances. We expect our ministrations in this hothouse environment to be the impetus for long-term behavior change. Training is a concentrated experience. That doesn't mean it can't be fun, interesting, or engaging. And that doesn't mean training should have the grind-them-down aura of medical or law school. It *does* mean that the laws of behavior, whatever those are this week, have a heightened — not diminished — effect in the training room.

Dumb Assumption #2: *Trainees have nothing to lose and everything to gain from a training experience.*

We routinely tell trainees to relax. It's OK to screw up during training. No one will hold anything you say or do against you. *Horse hockey!*

We all know what can happen back on the job to the trainee who is too self-revealing or confronting or candid or secretive or ill-tempered or aggressive or passive or obtuse or cunning or slow witted. In addition to the respect and goodwill of the 10 or 20 other people in the training session, trainees have their self-esteem and ego on the line every time they open their mouths. There are real things to lose — as well as gain — during training.

Dumb Assumption #3: *The trainer is a neutral source, clearly seen as above and beyond the organization's political fray.*

Somehow we have developed this sense that we are not a part of the social context of the training experience. We believe that as "facilitators of the learning experience" we are at the same time a high-powered stimulus for change and a neutral object. Can't have it both ways. We either affect people's behavior or we don't. Five years ago a guy in a half-day seminar I was running fed me one of those "Wouldn't you agree..." lines intended to make the questioner seem as smart or smarter than the presenter. I pounced on it like a hungry trout at a fly fishing convention. I got a laugh that Don Rickles would have envied. I see the guy around town all the time, but he hasn't spoken to me since that day my mouth ran off without my brain. But I'm told he has spoken of me in his company, and not exactly in glowing terms.

We may not control any significant long-term rewards or sanctions for our trainees, but the immediate and certain nature of the short-term consequences we do control give us more power than most of us care to admit.

If you're wondering what this diatribe is all about, or saying, "Who didn't know the training room is a part of — not apart from — the real world," I beg your indulgence. But, if you're like me, you need to be reminded once in a while that trainees' lives are greatly affected by what goes down in the training experience. They aren't just an audience. This isn't simply entertainment. And this ain't television or the movies. This is the real thing — life its own self. ■

The Group Facilitator's Role Is Easy — Until It Ain't

J ane is a friend of a friend. She is a bright, hard charging, highly ambitious midlife career changer who dropped into law school 11 years after finishing her MBA and a lengthy run as a marketing manager. She's one of those people who occasion thoughts of a long nap after you've spoken with them for 20 minutes. If you're envisioning someone strong, forceful, and not easily intimidated, you've captured the essential Jane.

So the nature of her phone call to me, one of those, "Am I crazy or is there something wrong with this picture?" inquires, was a surprise. The situation she described was even more so.

In a course on legal ethics Jane was taking, the professor split the class into little "firms" and gave each partner in each firm a set of assignments to carry out. From Jane's description, the assignments seem to have been constructed to create conflicts. The student/partners had, ultimately, to choose between completing a task for a fellow partner or finishing an assignment for a customer/client. Jane, who had worked for a very customer-focused company in her previous work life, chose clients over comrades and, in effect, left several of those comrades in her firm in a hypothetical lurch.

Efforts to transfer power hit a wall if facilitation and conflict management skills aren't improved in lockstep.

Here's where the plot thickens. Upon revelation that she had chosen clients over colleagues, Jane's playmates exploded...all over her. Voices were raised, recriminations flew and a couple of permanent vents appeared in the law school social fabric. A member of Jane's study group announced loudly that Jane was "obviously not to be trusted to act for the common good."

After hearing her tale, I was sure it would be my turn in the barrel and my task to defend "customer first" thinking in light of the adverse effects Jane had experienced. But her question was far more astute. Asked Jane: "The professor just sat there and watched. Shouldn't she have done something? This was supposed to be a learning experience, so I tried something that didn't work. Shouldn't she have kept it from ruining my reputation among my colleagues?"

An Absence of People Skills

If you've been around the training game for more than three minutes, and take seriously the dynamics of group work, you know better than I the answer to Jane's query: Hell yes, Jane's prof should have intervened. A rookie facilitator — even one with no more empathy skills than the average law school professor — would know better than to let Jane be cornered like that.

At the very least, the prof should have diverted the anger with a simple "Jane seems to have taken a different approach than Spot and Puff did. Can anybody else offer some insight into the two different approaches?" With any savvy at all she could have called time out and summarized what she saw happening. Instead, as Jane described it, "She sat there and smiled, as if somehow I was getting what I deserved."

Poor Facilitators Do Untold Harm

Jane's experience doesn't seem to be an aberration. A few weeks ago I was talking with an HRD director — call him George — who was more than a little miffed at the total quality "gurus" in his company. Said George: "They are insisting that everyone work in teams — whether that's appropriate or not — but they don't know a thing about group dynamics or managing conflict. Things are so balled up that the systems people aren't talking with branch operations, marketing isn't speaking with logistics, and no one in community affairs is speaking — period." The crux, as George went on to explain it: "The quality people not only don't know how to teach conflict management, they take sides when disagreement breaks out in a team. They think their job is to decide who's right and who's wrong." George isn't the first person I've heard from with some version of this complaint, that this stuff we do looks so easy *anyone* can do it.

At the core of George's frustration — and to an extent Jane's as well — seems to be the growing gap in the evolving workplace between means and ends. We've done a fabulous job of convincing management that less top-down control and more self-determination leads to improved productivity and better quality. Unfortunately, we've forgotten these new work structures — empowerment, teams, flexiblity, self-direction — require more sophisticated process skills than people generally have been called on to exercise in the workplace.

It would be too bad if the workplace revolution we are helping to ferment failed, not for lack of subscription, but for lack of skills; or a lack of means to achieve the ends we've already agreed on. ■

Gen X:
All Skilled Up
With No Place to Go

The glowing review in *The Wall Street Journal* of Charles Heckscher's book *White Collar Blues: Management Loyalties in an Age of Corporate Restructuring*, had lured me out of the office and into a nearby bookstore to find a copy.

After locating the Heckscher book and another "must read" I found — Jean Philippe Deschamp's and P. Ranganath Nayak's *Product Juggernauts* — I dropped them on the checkout counter. A primly-dressed, 20-something cashier gave my purchases a quizzical inspection. "What's a juggernaut?" she asked. I mumbled my way through an answer: "I think it has to do with being relentlessly good. The word comes from World War I; they described big battleships of that era as 'juggernauts.' "

She got that same look again as she ran the barcode reader over the *White Collar* book. "White collar blues — I've heard of that," she said. "What's it really about?"

I gave her my best approximation of the authoritative pundit look and held forth: "I don't know. That's why I bought it. But according to a review I read it's supposedly about mid-

> *"After so many years of school, it'd be nice to have an important job to worry about keeping."*

dle managers feeling betrayed and anxious about all the downsizing and reengineering that is going on in corporations. And that they'd better get used to it."

The cashier turned a sidelong glance on her coworker at the next register over and waved the book at him. "This is about nervous middle managers griping about their lives."

"We should have those problems, " the coworker observed dryly.

"Yeah, we should," she returned, with a tone that referenced more than a few commiserating career frustration conversations between them.

I remarked that it didn't seem they had much sympathy for the plight of these managers.

Said the cashier: "After so many years of going to school, it'd be nice to have an important job to worry about trying to keep." Then she retreated to the busy work of running my credit card and bagging my purchases.

A Demotivated Workforce

I found it ironic that I had planned on spending the day looking into the plight of the old-time manager in the brave new world of team management and volatile corporate structures, and instead found myself confronted with something infinitely more interesting and ultimately more troubling: the demotivation of an entirely different generation of workers.

They're called X-ers, those 20-something workers. They are that duet behind the counter at Barnes & Noble bookstore. Young, educated, once-hopeful wannabes trained and socialized to take their place in a work and lifestyle system that no longer exists. And fast becoming discouraged about ever catching a train for someplace more interesting.

The popular press does little to buoy their spirits or improve our second-hand image of Generation X. A recent widely publicized Gallup poll concluded that Xers have little loyalty toward employers, are more interested in quality of life than career advancement, and are four times as likely than 50-something managers (and twice as likely as Boomers) to call in sick when they are actually feeling quite well.

And while there is nothing sacrosanct about survey findings, we've heard more than a few stories of Xers giving trainers fits in the workplace and reinforcing that media stereotype. Here's the latest: An Xer college trainee comes sauntering into class at 10:45 a.m. The class, a six-month work-study program for new college graduates, runs from 8:30 a.m. to 5:30 p.m. Monday through Wednesday. "Welcome to Monday, Mr. Lo," chides the division head who was speaking on division strategy. Without missing a beat the trainee shot back, "My culture has a different time sense than yours, sir. You'll have to learn to respect that," and continued on to his seat.

Subversion...or Reasonable Behavior?

In the context of corporate culture and the rules of work and advancement as you and I learned them, that is unconscionable behavior. It's usually rewarded with a quick trip to an outplacement office and a big fat pink slip. But in light of today's real corporate world, and the rules of its new, hard-edge survival mentality, perhaps sick days and "clocks ain't in my culture, man" are, in fact, reasonable, if not rational behavior.

If, as Heckscher observes in *White Collar Blues*, "Loyalty comes with trust and believing, and this practice has largely been cast out across the whole of companies as being *not* the way to run things," then perhaps Xers' beliefs and suspicions – and their behavior as well — make even more sense than do yours or mine.

Ask my friends at Barnes & Noble, or their counterparts in your life. Then ask yourself this: What is your training function, and your organization, doing to create an alternative reality — a more positive reality where trust and commitment are more than hollow concepts — than the one Generation Xers seem to be bracing themselves for? ■

Beyond the 20-Somethings: Basic Skills Shortfall Will Soon Be Trainers' Problem

A related pair of news reports should give corporate trainers cause for pause. The first, a 1995 news story that has been trumpeted widely by conservative radio talk show hosts as a sign of the end of civilization as we know it, came to my attention via *The Atlanta Constitution*.

It seems that Fred Ayres, owner of Ayres Corp. in Albany, GA, a manufacturer of helicopters and airplane parts, has a pressing need for sheet metal workers. Ayres set out to hire and train 75 recent high school grads for the jobs, but to his surprise and dismay, he has been able to locate only 17 youngsters qualified to enter the training program among the hundreds of high school graduates interviewed and tested. "I get high school graduates and they can't understand fractions, work with decimals or read a simple blueprint. It looks like they've just been warehoused for 12 years and given a diploma just for showing up," Ayres told the Atlanta paper.

Generation X's younger siblings are not keeping pace.

As remarkable as those circumstances may or may not be in our strange new world, they are not nearly as remarkable as the reaction of that county's associate school superintendent, Alfredo Stokes. Asked to comment on the Ayres situation, Stokes said, in essence, that finishing high school doesn't guarantee that someone can read, write, or use basic math skills to an employer's satisfaction. His exact quote: "High school is just an interim level of education." He did not elaborate as to between what and where it is a waystation.

No Isolated Problem

A few days later we learned this is hardly an isolated incident. According to *The New York Times*, a massive new study finds that most employers long ago gave up hope that high school graduates are qualified for any but the most skill-free of jobs. The study, conducted by the National Center on the Educational Quality of the Work Force at the University of Pennsylvania, found that only one in five employers believe their employees to be proficient in their jobs, and that they don't just hire anyone right out of school. Instead, the study's authors say, "They wait until they are 26 years old, and then they'll look at them."

An odd footnote: The U of Penn researchers were, it seems, also surprised to find that when employers need to go outside to train the precious few proficient employees already on their staffs, they are more likely to turn to equipment manufacturers or consultants than to "established educational institutions" for that advanced training.

In California, I believe they call that a "duh!"

In days gone by, we might have shrugged and said something glib about how the fast-food industry could certainly take on more of these workers not skilled enough to toil at other companies.

But a manager I recently talked to in a Wendy's restaurant advises the times are a changin', and even those jobs now have more prerequisites. "Oh, we have jobs, and there are bodies out there," the manager said, "just not the right bodies. We need people who can think quickly and have a 'service heart' — not the bored and unwilling."

At another fast food firm, Taco Bell, crew members are cross-trained for most jobs, and do profit and loss statements for the store. According to CEO John Martin, the company believes it can no longer afford employees who aren't skilled, bright, and "empowerable."

A Shaky Future

If one times three still equals three (my computer has a Pentium chip, so I'm just guessing here) then there are several ponderables in these news-wire tea leaves, not the least of which is that our future appears to be in questionable hands. We've been hearing for some time that there is a 20-something generation hanging around the workplace that is difficult to manage, challenging to motivate, and whose members are very set in their views of work — they don't want to lead, follow, or be on duty after 5 p.m. But for all of that, they are, for the most part, smart, skilled, and quite good at their chosen vocations. As a legal firm talent scout told me the other day, "Thank God I'm recruiting them and not competing against them."

It is something of a jolt, however, to learn that Generation X's younger brothers and sisters, rather than being yet another step along the evolutionary trail toward smarter, faster and better, are actually a step back. How else do you define kids who can't read, write, or figure well enough to determine whether a number 7 can of cling peaches on sale for 10% off is a better or worse deal than a number 10 can at 8% off?

My concern, and I hope it is yours as well, is that those same said kids are downstairs right now in your personnel office trying to figure out how to fill out your company's job application form. Your company may be able to avoid hiring them today, tomorrow, or next week, but much sooner than later these skill-short young people are going to be through the gate and into your training rooms.

And unless I miss my guess, neither of us have a clue about how you turn them into happy, productive corporate citizens. Have a nice day. ■

Doom III: Honing the Skills for Tomorrow's Workforce

Managers across the country are in a collective snit over their employees' use of computer games. According to articles in *The Wall Street Journal* and *The New York Times,* managers are working along with computer support functions to block employee access to such deadly productivity menaces as *Solitaire®, Hearts* and *Minesweeper®.*

At the New Jersey Department of Environmental Protection, for example, employee attempts to call up these pernicious games are met with the message, "Sorry, department policy prohibits the use of this program."

The governor of the Commonwealth of Virginia has also banned game playing on all state-owned computer equipment. Violators of the ban are required to spend two hours viewing videotapes of the Oliver North/Chuck Robb senatorial campaign debates. This is serious stuff.

I know this to be a real concern for private sector employers as well. Just the other day my recommendation that a company's service technicians be supplied laptop computers was rebuked for just this reason. "Oh, ha," argued Mr. Rooney, head of customer service for Megakilo Byte Computers. "All we need is for those guys to sit around playing *Space Aliens®* all day."

> *A case can be made that, aside from being cost-effective stress relievers, computer games also hone a variety of important job-related skills.*

I didn't bother to tell him that nobody plays *Space Aliens®* anymore, but I did argue that maybe people who repair million-dollar computer systems could be trusted not to goof off like that — even though computer games are well known to be at least as addictive as crack cocaine and twice as dangerous to national security (you have seen the movie *War Games,* haven't you?) Anyway, Mr. Rooney, who himself had once carried a tool bag for a living, said that since he has "been there" he knew better than I just how much technicians could be trusted, which in his opinion is not at all.

The Redeeming Value of Games

Before someone goes and recommends that your company invest in a software package that can detect an employee two time zones away attempting to call up an unauthorized file of *Doom III®* — or worse yet, entice an innocent coworker into a game of remote contract bridge — I would like to say a word on behalf of computer game playing on company time. Playing computer games on a regular basis, and with discretion, is not only a very cost-effective stress and boredom reliever — and a viable alternative to the 10-minute cof-

fee break — it has cognitive skill enhancement value as well. I am totally serious here.

If you are in the health care or city government business, you are already aware of the value of commercial off-the-shelf simulations like *SimHealth* and *SimCity*®. The simulation game *Themepark*® isn't a bad exercise in how to run a company — and enjoyable as well. But I contend that even the "game games," the kind your kids play and you sneak a peek at when they're in bed, have important educational value.

I know that the hours friends and I have logged in a microsimulated cockpit of a 747 that is circumventing the globe – and occasionally crash landing at international airports — have been experientially valuable and a lot cheaper than a trip to one of those off-in-the-woods, down-the-roaring- rapids retreats. And much more comfortable.

Minesweeper®, *Solitaire*® and *Myst*® all hone attention to detail, logical thinking, and deductive reasoning of even the least-skilled of players. *Network Hearts* promotes wonderful lessons in team effort and forming temporary alliances. And don't even get me started on the intellectual and business value of playing computer bridge or chess.

It's in the Way that You Use It

Let me conclude this exposition of the other side of the story by reminding you that a thing isn't always what it appears to be so far as educational value is concerned — especially in the training and development world. Tinkertoys ain't just tinkertoys when they become part of an exercise in team cooperation. A blindfold is no longer just part of a kid's game when it's put in a diversity facilitator's skilled hands. And a good cigar — well, see Sigmund Freud about that.

Gotta run...I've got a hot date with *Mortal Kombat*®. ■

Using Causes As Cudgels

An old friend contends that no good deed ever goes unpunished. I don't think the sentiment is original with her, but it seemed all too apt one day last week as I worked my way through a micro-flurry of less-than-laudatory mail from readers. These are the kind with greetings that begin "You Moron" or "Someone in your position should know better than to..." and that end, "This is not a letter to the editor [which explains its viciousness] but feel free to call me so that I may further educate you on this vital issue!"

My moronic misdeed was to use politically incorrect and insensitive language in an editorial reminding customer service managers to make sure their offices, stores, products and services are easily accessible and user-friendly to people with handicaps and older, less-abled customers and consumers. The column, and an accompanying question-and-answer piece about barriers and obstacles, ran in Lakewood Publications' *The Service Edge* newsletter. Both were occasioned by a couple of outstanding presentations I'd encountered at recent training and customer service conferences. It seemed like a heck of an important idea to relay, from both a business and human spirit perspective. And to tell the truth, I did indeed feel I'd done a "Right Thing."

Ha! For my efforts I've received nothing but bile-tinged upbraidings.

Had I asked her, Beverly Geber, associate editor with *TRAINING Magazine*, could have waved me off the topic. In the December 1990 issue of *TRAINING* she wrote an outstanding piece on what enlightened employers are doing to accommodate people with disabilities in the workplace ("The Disabled: Ready, Willing and Able"), a piece that was cited by the Bush Administration with an American Business Press Association's "Points of Light" Award. You'd have never known from her mailbag, though, that she'd written an article destined to be so honored. She got a healthy handful of letters on that article — nearly all of them berating her for failing to use the term "people with disabilities" and questioning how this publication could afford such a lout on its payroll.

All of which makes me wonder: If this is how people concerned about equality for people with disabilities treat their friends, how do they deal with the untrusting, the uncaring and the reluctant? Or the downright hostile?

Of course, it's not fair to single out advocates for people with disabilities. Everywhere we turn today causes are being used as cudgels. These weapons are permanently cocked instruments of persuasion in some unnamed power game wherein any infraction of the rules — rules defined primarily by the cudgel wielder — constitutes sufficient grounds for full frontal assault on the infraction and on the character of the committer. Friends of the family receive no exclusions.

All that notwithstanding, I would have eagerly penned some face-saving saccharine mea culpa for writing "physically disabled customers" and "blind passenger," instead of "customers with physical disabilities" and "passenger who is visually challenged," had it not been for one writer who also tore at me for quoting the wrong expert — namely an expert who was not the letter writer himself.

With that, it finally hit me. I was looking at causes from the point of view of their content and had completely ignored the more important part: their politics. At long last I understood the purpose of righteous indignation — it is about power and control, not about plight or dignity or acceptance. It is about who gets to say what is right and wrong, not about what is right and wrong.

It's About Politics, Not Content

I am left feeling, well, embarrassed. The kind of annoyed-at-yourself embarrassed I suspect we all feel when we realize we've been playing by different rules than the insiders. It is the feeling of foolishness we all share when we realize we've erred in expecting a thing to be neither more nor less than it purports to be. Like expecting members of Congress, who give themselves raises because of the "heavy expenses" they incur representing us in Washington, to actually have expenses.

It is the same feeling I had when I was 12, and I learned that those shiny, swift soapbox racers I so admired weren't built by the kids driving them, but by their fathers. Sometimes, they were even built by a syndicate of their fathers' engineer and mechanic and cabinetmaker friends. Somehow, that made it about as interesting to stand at the bottom of the hill rooting for the kid from Kokomo to triumph over the guy from Grand Rapids as to watch the outcome of a professional wrestling tag-team match.

And it's too bad you and I are developing that sense of cynicism. Too bad for the good people and good causes. Too bad for those of us who simply want to feel we've participated in something worthwhile and helpful. Too bad for the politics and politicians of our day, who are expecting us to "read their lips" and believe that what we see is what we'll get.

Cynicism is infectious, but not nearly as infectious as the guile that incubates it. ■

CHAPTER 2

THE INFLUENTIAL TRAINING LEADER

INTRODUCTION

The New World
of the Training Manager

From time to time I've mused to myself that working in training is a superior way to make a living. Think about it. You get to stand up in front of a room full of people, tell jokes and relate anecdotes, raise aggravating points of view, facilitate heated discussions — and even break up food fights. If there's any of the circuit-riding preacher in your soul, you've got to believe that training is the most fun you can have with all your clothes on.

And even if your brand of training runs less to stand-up delivery and more toward computer-delivered instruction, video creation, facilitation, or slogging it out in the trenches of performance analysis, it is a great kick to be out there doing your thing full time, trying to win one for the Gipper, your ego, and maybe, just maybe, making a little bit of difference.

And you get paid for it. And most of you get paid rather well, to boot. Now, don't start. I see the numbers you've been sending in for *TRAINING Magazine's* annual salary survey since 1982, and even though increases have been light the last few years, you're still ahead of the curve.

Keeping Training Managers from Their 'True Love'

But it would be nice if you ever actually got to do a little training or problem analysis or strategy facilitation. At least that's the lament I increasingly hear from my training manager friends. At the root, there are several culprits. The first is the time-honored Peter Principle gone mad. You went and got pretty darn good at something, whether it be standup, performance consulting, or building multimedia modules. And some booby came along and offered you a box full of money and the word "manager" after your name. And from that point forward, you seldom — if ever — are engaged in a meaningful way in the thing you've proven you can do well. And the thing that often is your true love.

But even if you have consistently said "no" to the upward spiral toward managerhood, there is no guarantee you will actually ever be able to do very much of what you are very good at. (Or don't they have meetings where you work?)

One of my partners delivers roughly 90 speeches a year. The talk he gives in San Diego for World Wide Widgets is pretty much the same speech he'll give the day after to the Flower Flockers of Florida in Orlando. But for every hour of presentation, there are eight more of talking and listening to words of wisdom about the uniqueness and special concerns that make the Golden Rod Harvesters like no other group on earth, and the Fan Belt Distributors unlike any other industry.

An approximation of that same dialogue often goes on when you are an in-house training manager:

"Turlick, we'll need to carefully consider this competency-building plan of yours. After all, selling wallpaper is a unique and special talent that not everyone has. I can tell you from my long years as a coverings man that there are a lot of intangibles and subtleties here. A real wall-treatment person is born, not trained."

There is also a new twist these days that makes the whole thing maddeningly slower than a tree sloth on a cold day: call it SODM, or Suspension of Decision-Making. The newly downsized workplace means not only that the front-line training troops have more to do and less incentive to do it, but that members of management are exposed like never before to the glare of their individual actions. And that has led to a psychological syndrome some are calling FOBW, or Fear of Being Wrong, which begets a behavior pattern characterized by endless nitpicking, senseless meetings, stalling, backpeddling, and decision reversal. Or SODM for short.

Actually, it makes perfect sense, in a Dilbert sort of way. Decision-making researchers say that the more we know about a situation — the more data we have — the longer we take to make a decision, and the less comfortable we are with the decision we make. So you would indeed be a bit suspect if you were a senior training manager who actually made a decision today without being backed into a corner and threatened with loss of life, limb, and parking space.

Facing New Challenges

Challenging training managers even further are trends toward outsourcing the time famine in companies, using technology-delivered instruction, and an increased expectation to show training's impact on the bottom line.

Rather than managing a training department with full-time designers or instructors, you are more often managing relationships with a handful of outside vendors or a corps of "contract" trainers. All of which requires new skill sets, like how to negotiate cost-effective and airtight contracts, and how to manage and motivate a free-lance workforce.

You are expected to make informed decisions on a dizzying array of multimedia authoring systems, electronic performance support options, and Web-based delivery products. You are asking long-time instructors to make the often-painful conversion to "performance consulting" or to teach to a camera rather than to a classroom, when many would rather accept a long needle in the eye.

So, submitted to comfort you on this treadmill journey are the following essays and idea-starters about the nature of managing workers and work in the wonderful new world of training and development. — **R.Z.**

Tough Times and Rising Demands Test Training's Ability to 'Just Say No'

ncreasingly, these hard economic times are putting pressure on the quality of our training. Hard times teach hard — and occasionally surprising — lessons, and one we've got to be especially leery of is coming up embarrassingly short of our own claims.

Case in point from an issue of *The Wall Street Journal*: James Brecht is director of the international marketing department for Graco Inc., a Minnesota pump manufacturer. Last June he was scheduled to do a few days work in Japan, then go on to Taiwan for important meetings with 10 new customers. But his two-and-a-half-hour flight from Japan to Taiwan turned into an 18-hour flight back to Minneapolis. The reason? A travel agent at Carlson Travel Network had forgotten to advise Brecht he needed a visa to enter Taiwan.

Don't let your neck get stiff from nodding 'yes' to every knee-jerk training proposal you hear.

At the root of this slipup is a set of circumstances that should unsettle managers and trainers in any organization. According to Carlson managers, the company has been on a campaign to raise productivity and control costs. Part of that effort involved cutting 17 percent of its travel agents and retraining the survivors to handle a broader range of responsibilities.

Yep, you guessed it. One of those retrained agents handled Brecht's ill-fated trip. It was her first international booking — ever. As *The WSJ* quotes her: "I think learning new things is really a good challenge, but I was overwhelmed."

By its own admission, Carlson's management learned the hard way that improving productivity, quality, service, or profits is more difficult than simply solving for "X" in some straightforward business school "hours x dollars = returns" formula.

Behind that lesson there is also a warning for training managers everywhere: Don't let your mouth make promises your training can't keep. Not your style? Well, OK. But take this three-question quiz before you dismiss the warning out of hand.

Question #1:

You are face-to-face with the VP of order taking and complaint handling. "I've got to eliminate the third shift," he/she says. "I figure we bring in part of the first shift early and hold part of the second shift late. You can train 'em to handle the extra load, right?"

Do you: (A) Pull the trigger and tell this VP what you think of his/her idea? (B) Nod your head up and down like one of those little plastic dogs with the light-up eyes you used to see in the back windows of tooled up '57 Chevys?

Question #2:

Your new telephone sales training program has a great pilot test. Trained operators outsell untrained by 30 percent. "Super," says the head of the outbound center. "But the training is too long. Can't you cut all the role-playing and observing and monitoring? Just do the lectures and show the film. Those have all the need-to-know stuff."

Do you: (A) Explain the downside of cutting those activities and stand your ground; (B) Find a way to shift more of the observe-and-practice to the supervisors; or (C) Nod your head up and down like one of those little plastic dogs with the light-up eyes that...?

Question #3:

A new product is going into manufacture. Plant management will shift 80 percent of the people on the "standard" line to the new product and replace them with temps, due to a hiring freeze. You find out management wants standard line employees to spend one shift training the temps, then report to the new product line where engineers will train them on the "ins and outs" of running the new line.

Do you: (A) Voice your concerns about the quality and duration of this training? (B) Nod your head up and down...?

How to Score this Quiz

If your neck is stiff from nodding, you probably know how painfully "at risk" your organization is. If you are a little uncomfortable, but still feel in control, congrats — you're ahead of the game. If you're positive you've never been co-opted by management, seduced into substituting a "once over lightly" orientation for real training, or haven't backed off on your demand for refresher training for people who are asked to take on responsibilities they haven't been near in a couple of years, then you should feel pretty good.

But just in case, it wouldn't hurt to get a copy of the Carlson story from *The WSJ*, fold it up, and put it in your date book. If you can reread it and still pat yourself on the back, fax me your claim for a shiny Susan B. It'll be my pleasure to pay up and listen to you crow about the secrets of your success. ■

Balancing Your Inner Voice with the Cacophony of the Customer

I n his autobiography, Chuck Jones, the creative father of cartoon characters Pepé Le Pew, Wile E. Coyote, and the Road Runner — and stepfather of Bugs Bunny, Daffy Duck, Elmer Fudd, and Porky Pig — makes this observation about market research:

"I make cartoons for me. This wasn't always true. In my more intellectual youth I tried studying audiences — making notes and timing their laughs. But the more I learned about audiences, the worse my cartoons grew."

Jones goes on to write that, once he gave up trying to please anyone but himself, his cartoons began to evoke laughter.

It is tempting to point to successes like Jones' and declare the "self set" course the best. And in truth, it is a workable strategy — 80% of the time. After all, Steve Jobs and Bill Gates and Warren Buffet and Mary Kay Ash became living business legends by setting their own visions, keeping their own counsels, and listening to the beat of their own unique, idiosyncratic drums.

Creativity comes not from unlimited license but from the narrow bounds of opportunity.

Well, yes and no. No, none of these self-made billionaires went out and ran focus groups to help develop their visions of what might be barn-burning business ideas. But neither did they ignore completely the response and reaction of the world around them to their ideas. And today, as they go about the never-ending business of refining and reinventing the products and services that have made them rich and famous, they all lean heavily on their audiences, associates, and sundry experts for input to that continual improvement.

The difference between inspired creation and pandering lies not in how successfully the creative few ignore all but their own personal muse, but in how they use the reactions of their audiences to the multitude of trial balloons they float, to the failures and successes of their prototypes, and to the sharpening of their visions of what might be possible.

They also tend to be flexible in the use of input they glean — and grateful for its occurrence. They understand customer feedback that says, "The widgets I own now are just fine — I have no use for your next-generation version of them," presents a whole different challenge than input saying "it would be better if your widgets were red, or if they were easier to use."

That flexibility is called judgment — using what helps, ignoring what doesn't, and having a clear feeling for which is which.

Training: One of Many Possible Solutions

Judgment is as important in training as it is in managing software products, cosmetics, or creating animated cartoons. The client who pronounces, "What we need around here is some communications training," may or may not know what he is talking about. But you can afford neither to ignore his clinical instinct nor blindly adhere to his dictates. Only your patient listening, careful questioning and — in the last analysis — your professional judgment can turn a training need expressed into a problem solved.

Creativity comes not from unlimited license and a blank page, but from understanding clearly the narrow bounds of opportunity that exist within every problem — and finding an eloquent solution that fits those conditions.

So what about the contrary Mr. Jones, our aforementioned cartoon creator? Later in his book he describes a four-step process that was at the core of all of his cartoon story creations. In the second of these steps, three directors, three writers, a producer and the production chief sat together and held what Jones described as a "Yes Session."

Warming Rays & Cold Shoulders

"This was not a brainstorming session in the usual sense — it was a 'yes' session, not an 'anything goes' session. Anything went, but only if it was positive, supportive, and affirmative to the premise of 'no negatives allowed,'" 59Jones writes.

The outcome of these two-hour sessions, Jones says, was an idea that either immediately excited the assembled and lived, or was met with stony silence and died. Only those proposals that passed professional muster with this most knowledgeable audience of Jones' peers survived the trail from mind's eye to the mighty silver screen.

The message? In the end, even the creative genius of Chuck Jones benefited from the warming rays and cold shoulders of that most precious of informational products — the opinions of others. ■

Little Lies: Without Care, They Can Empty Our Souls of All Good Intentions

S ir Ian McKellen is a renowned British actor currently touring North America playing the title role in Shakespeare's *Richard the III*. Sir Ian is also gay. Claims he has been for 49 of his 53 years. In a recent interview he explained why he gave up his "secret" in 1988. Among the words he chose to explain were "sense of self," "respect for relationships," and "honesty." But nothing he said then or since was more eloquent and to the point than this: "It is an obscenity when society forces people to lie about themselves for fear of losing their jobs or public position."

Reading that interview in my local newspaper called up for me the memory of a 1971 black comedy called *Little Murders*. It is a gritty sort of flick, funny, a little macabre, and easy to identify with. It's about the "little big things" of life that drain our energy and empty our souls of will and pride and joy, and turn us into unhappy paranoids walking about with loaded guns and empty hearts. It's about traffic jams, broken elevators, cancelled meetings, urban jungle, violence and hate in the streets, discord at home and work, no time, no fun, no sense of accomplishment, a life of knowing there will always be dog poop on your shoes — if not today then tomorrow.

> 'Going along' can smooth rocky waters, but in the long run the practice will sink your moral ship.

But *Little Murders* is about more than the inconveniences of place and space. It is also about the "little big" intangibles that lead to spirit death. Things like giving in to the pressure to "go along to get along." And that's why I thought of this movie when I read McKellen's words. He's talking about the biggest little murder of them all — the conscious conspiratorial lie. The shared lie. The deception that no one believes...nor disputes...and thereby everyone quietly endorses. It is the politically comfortable lie that makes the status quo so cozy.

We disagree but we go along out of weariness and desire to fit in. It's the decision to keep quiet because, "It's her money!" or "It's their company!"

There is another way. In his book, *The Truth Option* (Ten Speed Press, 1984), psychologist Will Schutz calls truth telling "the great simplifier," and observes, "I do not pursue truth because it is good or moral or spiritual or right. I simply observe what happens to me and my relationships when I tell more truth than usual."

About lying, he says, "Not telling the truth induces stress. This stress includes the energy required for lying; the need to remember the lie, as well as to whom I told it; the concern over being caught; the worry that someone will reveal my lie; the tension of facing someone who knows I am lying; the anxiety over whether or not someone else is lying; and the conflicts with my moral or religious beliefs."

Lots of us see this complicity as simply a way to get things done, as grease in the industrial wheels, a normal part of "taking care of business." But not Schutz. He doesn't see telling the truth as a final desperate option. It's purifying, annealing, and healing.

Writes Schutz: "This discovery was shocking, because I always assumed that I had to be strategic, judicious, discreet, and selective about the truth I tell. But to my surprise, I found that not telling the truth is the source of most problems. My personal relations are more vital when I am totally honest. When I go to work it seems that about 80 percent of all my problems are not real problems at all. They are simply the result of not telling the truth, of lying or withholding."

Sometime today — it happens every day — you and I will be face-to-face with a boss, a line customer, a trainee, a colleague, a child, or a spouse with a difficult question. There is always an easy answer. But there is also always the alternative, a harder, truthful answer — an answer that may not feel as good to deliver, or that may not make us look good, or may cause anger or sadness or disappointment. It may be an answer that will hurt rather than save feelings, an answer that may risk a relationship or a project or even a job. But we need to think, for a moment at least, about the real cost of walking too often along that more tempting, more comfortable course.

There is the cost in lost self-regard, and the cost of diminished hope of ever again being open or honest with the person you've deceived. There is the cost of the control that opting for the easy untruth will ever after exert on you. And there is the toll taken on your basic humanity.

Knowing what is true from what is false and risking to tell the truth is basic to what defines us as human, is it not? Telling the truth binds us together more tightly with other people than anything else, does it not? And aren't McKellen and Schutz right? Isn't it the ultimate obscenity to give up that right of humanity and humanness knowingly, and cavalierly, and without a struggle? ■

Is Training a Profession?

*T*RAINING got a letter recently from a fellow who took issue with our practice of referring to human resources development as a profession. " 'HRD Profession' is an oxymoron," he protested. "I acknowledge that HRD sports much of the paraphernalia of a profession. Practitioners write books and articles, form associations, hold meetings, read papers and publish journals. But the meat of professionalism is absent. HRD practitioners have no professional standards, don't engage in disciplined standards, and don't hold members accountable for writing and speaking arrant nonsense."

Laying aside the observation that the writer may be confusing "profession" with "science," the challenge has merit. What constitutes a profession? And when judged by that standard, how fares the pot-pourri of interests and practices we bundle together under the umbrella of HRD? The answer depends greatly upon the charity, clarity — and angle — of your view.

> *Nobody 'respects' lawyers, but that doesn't mean law isn't a profession.*

It would be hard to deny that there is, in fact, a calling, a vocation, a broadly defin-able category of employment engaged in by an identifiable body of persons and commonly referred to as human resources development. This group of paid practitioners embraces (after a fashion) a body of principles and practices aimed at helping individuals and groups perform jobs and tasks in a manner conducive to fulfilling the mission and aims of an enterprise. OK, it's not medicine or nuclear physics or law, but in this softest sense, this sense of a community of people engaged in common effort, HRD is a profession.

But is it a profession in the sense defined by *Webster's New Riverside University Dictionary*: "An occupation or vocation requiring training in the liberal arts or the sciences and advanced study in a specialized field?" Well, there is no central, certifying agency that "requires" a certain educational background for HRD practitioners. But landing a good job in the field without at least a master's degree is no picnic. To see why, we need look no further than this very magazine's demographics: 40 percent of *TRAINING's* subscribers are equipped with master's degrees, and another 7 percent hold doctorates.

Still, a profession is not a profession simply through self-declaration and the accident of numbers, despite the possible protestations of Professional Rattle Snake Milkers. Serious writers on the topic of what constitutes a profession generally agree on five criteria: an organized body of knowledge; client recognition of the authority of the profession; community approval of the profession's authority; a code of ethics; and a professional culture, supported and advanced by academic and association activities.

HRD seems to me to satisfy those criteria, though reasonable people could disagree about the extent to which it meets some of them: How "organized" is a body of knowledge that arguably encompasses everything from instructional design and performance technology to organization development and industrial psychology? Given trainers' penchant for complaining that they get no respect from management, to what degree can clients be said to recognize the field's authority? (Counterargument: Nobody respects lawyers, but that doesn't mean law isn't a profession.) Ethics? Well, we have to confess there are no codes of law that sanction particular courses of action in the HRD field, nor is there any equivalent of disbarment, license revocation or defrocking available for the censure of miscreant practitioners who speak "arrant nonsense."

Is HRD a profession? In the strictest of senses — the criteria derivable from, say, medicine, engineering, law or theology — we'd have to agree that the answer is no. In a broader sense, when laid against a scale stretching from real estate sales to neurosurgery, I would submit that HRD is at least comfortably right of center.

I suppose we could narrowly define which piece of the HRD pie we really want to talk about, and then count the number of institutions that grant Ph.D.s in the area, the number of refereed journals that print papers and research, and number of government departments threatening to regulate the field, fund its research, or study it as an economic entity. But I would apply as well a criterion struck upon by Anthony Jurkus, a management professor at Louisiana Tech University who set out to address the question, "Is management a profession?"

Jurkus assessed management against the five consensus requirements mentioned above. And at the end of his examination he concluded, "While management may not meet the standards as fully as the traditionally accepted profession, there is much evidence of professionalizing activity." Sound like a dodge? Maybe. But I like his approach. It's the effort to professionalize that counts — or, at least, that effort counts for a great deal.

In the past two years, *TRAINING*, *Training & Development* and *Performance & Instruction* have all run articles on the pros and cons of certification — a sign of a field moving toward professionalism. Look, too, at the massive efforts of associations like the American Society for Training and Development and the International Society for Performance Improvement to develop inclusive competency statements.

Maybe it is precisely this attempt to turn a loose confederacy of practices and practitioners into a stratified, codified profession that best defines HRD's professionalism. ■

Leaders: Special Attributes Help Them Thrive in Complex and Uncertain Times

Harlan Cleveland, former dean of the University of Minnesota's Humphrey Institute of Public Affairs, has led as stimulating and thought-provoking a life as one could imagine. He served as ambassador to NATO, administrator of the Marshall Plan, assistant secretary of state, and president of the University of Hawaii. He coined the term "revolution of rising expectations" to characterize the growing frustration of an increasingly materialistic world, and has been awarded the president's Medal of Freedom.

So I read with more than passing interest a recent piece of Cleveland's titled, "The Essence of Leadership in One Minute's Reading." Though the title pokes gentle fun at today's McManagement trend, it is a one-minute read of a lifetime's challenge. To me, it speaks simple but eloquently not of the skills of leadership, but of the prerequisites; the attitudes and attributes, and perhaps the basic personality necessary in managers who would lead, be they in the private or public sectors.

> *For a leader, life is more worth living when there is risk and a chance to project and mold the future.*

So, here, in slight synopsis, is Cleveland's arsenal of eight attitudes for leadership in a democracy. Or, as Cleveland himself puts it, the attributes "indispensable to the management of complexity," whenever that challenge may rear its head.

■ A *lively, intellectual curiosity; an interest in everything.*

In a complex world, things are inextricably intertwined. Everything is related, therefore everything is related to what you are doing. Inspiration and opportunity can come from anywhere.

■ A *genuine interest in what other people think and why they think the way they do.*

It's hard to fake an interest in others and their ideas. Being interested, really interested and willing to learn from others, regardless of their credentials, begins with being at peace with yourself. It's hard to get in touch with, learn from and build upon the strengths of those around you if you are constantly threatened by their ideas, abilities and accomplishments.

■ A *feeling of responsibility for envisioning a future that's different from a straight-line projection of the present.*

Real leaders have more zest for what might be than for what is, or even for seeing to completion what they have already started. Tomorrow is tabula rasa: a chance to begin again, to do even better than the last time, to create something truly different and perhaps perfect this time.

- *The attitude that risks are there not to be avoided, but to be taken.*

Great risk leads to great reward, or so thinks the leader. But there is more to it than a risk/reward-balance sheet. For a leader, life is more worth living at the tip of a surfboard on the crest of the wave; anything else is boredom and book work.

- *The feeling that crisis is normal, tensions can be promising, and complexity is fun.*

The leader doesn't really come fully alive without some sense of crisis, and hardly pays attention unless the situation is a bit arcane, vague and convoluted.

- *The realization that paranoia and self-pity are reserved for people who don't want to take the lead.*

Having ideas "borrowed" by others without attribution or seeing a competitor come up with a better solution to a problem doesn't turn the leader into a raving maniac. But then again it doesn't make him or her the most pleasant person to be around, either.

- *The quality of unwarranted optimism.*

Leaders seem to share a conviction that an upbeat outcome is always possible regardless of how hopeless or dismal the situation may look at the moment — if they could only think of how to get there.

- *A sense of personal responsibility for the general outcome of his or her efforts.*

Leaders believe their efforts matter, that what they do affects people and events and that they are, therefore, somehow responsible for what happens around them. They believe they make a difference.

At least walking on water didn't make Cleveland's list, but then again it simply might be subsumed under "unwarranted optimism."

Cleveland's armament of attitudes, his succinct description of a real leader's mindset, gave me cause for pause and chance for a little reflection. For one thing, it explained why in years gone by it has been so much easier to get up and go when I was working for one person, and so hard to hit the floor or feel good about what I was doing for another. It reminded me, too, why some causes and some crusades have seemed so much more important, urgent and winnable than have others; why so many of the would-be presidents parading across the nightly news seem such midgets in grown-up's shoes. And it reminded me why the world seems so much diminished when a real leader passes from it, and why we remember the light only from the darkness. ∎

Is Good Management Really Just Good Manners?

There we were, spread-elbowed around a dark corner table, sullenly guarding it against a sudden surge of anti-gravity, telling lies and grousing about pulling duty at yet another carbon-copy training conference.

"Yeah," agreed one or another of us, "as far as I can tell, every how-to-manage program in the world is just the same four or five ideas repackaged."

"Amen," said Jeannie Smith, a consultant from Alexandria, VA, and the table's self-appointed contrarian. "But what do you expect? After all, good management is just good manners, and there are only so many ribbons you can tie around that dear little box."

The soft side of management acumen may be little more than elaborate masquerade — courtesy dressed for success.

Encouraged by a reasonable number of guffaws, she pressed on. "Laugh if you want, but nothing I learned in graduate school — or at one of these conferences — has been as useful to me as my East Texas upbringing and the rules of tact and decorum my Southern mother taught me."

Good management and "effective interpersonal communication" as nothing but common courtesy and simple good manners? Well, it certainly is true that if you ignore the title and context, it's hard to tell *The Amy Vanderbilt Complete Book of Etiquette* from many a contemporary management text. For instance, here's Amy on what some like to call "positive feedback":

"One of the most gracious forms of communication is the paying of a compliment. It is an art. Children learn how to pay compliments by living in a household where the parents compliment other members of the family, their friends, and the people with whom they come in daily contact. Sons and daughters are influenced by the way in which their parents receive a compliment or automatically react to a situation by giving a compliment. A child who grows up in an environment where one is not afraid to express praise, where one does it to please others, but also to encourage and help them, will probably emulate his elders when he grows up."

It is probably too severe to suggest that the soft side of management science is little but an elaborate masquerade — courtesy and common sense dressed for success. Still, there's a mighty suspicious similarity. Witness this quote from an essay by W.H. Weiss in an issue of *The Effective Executive:*

"The successful leader understands people and knows how to get along with them. Two of the skills that help in working with people are tact and diplomacy....Tact concerns dealing with people without offending them....Diplomacy is closely related to tact in that it is a skill in handling affairs without raising antagonism or hostility."

So pardon me if I am tempted to drop into the same drawer every soft skills training idea from The Management Grid® through The Habits of 7 Highly Obnoxious People.

I'm tempted, but the problem with the drawer solution is one of context, assumptions and behavior. On the one hand, there are the "Theory Y" assumptions about people at work: that they are innately smart and skillful, and they'll try hard to do a good job. On the other hand, there is the real world where, despite the fact that most people may be smart and skillful and trying to do a good job, things go wrong.

Results First, Manners Second

No organization runs smoothly and conflict-free all the time — not Disney, not the Girl Scouts, and certainly not any organization I've ever worked in. In that context, "Please," "Thank you," and "Have a nice day" fall short of the people-handling savvy one needs to keep relative peace.

The workplace isn't a dinner party. A boor at a dinner party or a louse across the card table can be indulged for an evening and avoided in the future. Workplace relationships are less transient and trivial, and much more pressured. William Ouchi, author of Theory Z, marvels that organizations accomplish as much as they do. The idea of people working together on a sustained basis for a common purpose represents, he says, "an unnatural act requiring great will and orchestration."

It's also true that in the workplace, verbal brutality and bad manners often are tolerated, if not condoned when the offenders are individuals who make significant contributions to the hallowed bottom line. Heavy hitters don't get fired for talking with their mouths full, interrupting or failing to send bread-and-butter notes. In the workplace, even the truly boorish, the outrageously self-seeking and the just plain unpleasant of the world must be dealt with on a day-to-day basis. And as far as that goes, sometimes tact, diplomacy and a concern for mannerly behavior must be set aside in service to that for which one is held organizationally accountable.

Manners and tact then are a palliative that allows the stronger stuff to be accepted — and tolerated. If, like me, you secretly admire those few who seem always calm, cool, collected and ever so proper, it may be good to remember that the word "judo," literally translated, means "gentle way." And that implies nothing soft and squishy — simply that an iron hand works best in a carefully wielded velvet glove. ■

Morale: Assessing Your Own Will Give You a Good Read on the Troops

'd like a dollar for every time I've heard a manager — or a line employee — say, "The morale around here is lower than a snake's belly!" But, to tell you the truth, I've never taken the comment seriously, or at least literally. I've always reacted with a wisp of condescension, and a mental sidestep. And I may have been dead wrong to do so.

Tactically, in these cases, I've always asked some clever redirecting question like, "What is it you've seen employees do or heard them say that leads you to that conclusion?" Or I simply probed for a more operational description of the problem. I've always assumed — somewhat arrogantly — that words like "morale" are too general, too overused and too inexact to solve important organizational problems.

I recently listened to Bruce A. Baldwin discuss the relevance of morale to life in America and it turned my head. Baldwin, a clinical psychologist from Wilmington, NC, believes morale is a substantive issue that organizations have virtually ignored. "Morale isn't that complex," Baldwin holds. "It is simply the state of the relationship between an individual and an organization. That organization may be a country, a company or a family. The difficult part is that it is within the individual. It isn't a group-to-group thing so it isn't easy to observe. Its clues and cues are subtle. Since it isn't easy to observe, measure or talk about, we ignore it — or at least shy away."

How to Measure Morale

The "so what?" — the organizational importance — is that morale has an impact on productivity. It is certainly not a revelation to anyone in this field that the way people feel about their companies, jobs or careers has an impact on how hard they work, how long they stay and how much they produce. The theorem that "contented cows give more milk" is, after all, at the root of climate and attitude surveying.

Listening to Baldwin, I was reminded that it is the measurement and nurturance of morale that is the issue, not job satisfaction, confidence in supervision, scope of responsibility, or any of the indicators upon which we can fixate. And that, for me, is an important distinction. In an organizational intervention, it is probably more important to work on a number of fronts and not spend all your time on a single factor. Likewise, it suggests that interventions with individuals may even be more worthy a pursuit than flashy, group interventions.

Baldwin suggests we simplify our approach. Says he: "The first thing you have to do to get a handle on morale is to learn to look and listen to what's going on around you, but that takes time. You have to learn to distinguish between indicators of low morale and the basic BLB — the baseline bitching

RON ZEMKE **69**

that goes on in every organization."

For my part, I suggest we start with ourselves, using the litmus tests Baldwin proposes for sensing morale level.

1. Examine your sense of humor. Do you use joke telling and levity for tension relief or to safely express your frustration and cynicism about the organization? Are you cynical about the organization — especially about its commitment to employee training?

2. Listen to the grapevine. Listen to the messages you put the most stock in. Are they run of the mill who-is-getting-promoted-hired-fired-sleeping-with-whom sort of normal grapevine chatter, or scary stuff like, "This company is going down the tubes and those bozos in the front office don't give a damn!"

3. Look at your own health and wellness. Are you sick more often than you can remember being in the past? Lots of colds, headaches, flu bouts?

4. Examine your need for mental health days. We all have times when we just can't seem to get out of bed; when we need a day away from pressures of office, family, friends or any kind of expectation. Have the intervals between them been decreasing?

5. Look at your attrition rate. Are you losing good people? Sure, trainers tend to be transients, wanderers. But if the instructor you hired six months ago is whistling "Done laid around, done stayed around this old town too long...," it may be time to question your morale management.

6. Ask someone you trust about your griping. Have you become a complainer who sees the world as a series of unsolvable problems? And how do your employees talk about you behind your back?

7. Look at your responsiveness. Do you stall and delay meetings with other managers — your clients? Do you think of them as burdens instead of opportunities?

There's nothing magical in this assessment, but it is important to look at ourselves as early warning sensors in the matter of organizational morale. "Morale," says Baldwin, "reflects and reveals the heart of the organization." ∎

Even Your Best Trainers Never Outgrow the Need for Skillful Coaching

I t was one of those "Management 101" questions, one I've heard a thousand times. This time it was different, however. The questioner was a very successful, award-winning State Farm Insurance agent well known in parts of Georgia as a good boss and a good people developer. I would have weighed it differently had it been asked by a less-savvy manager.

His question: "I was walking through the office the other day and heard one of my people on the phone hassling with an old, longtime customer. When she hung up, I sat down and told her I'd heard the end of her conversation and asked if I could help in any way. We went through the whole scenario, and I talked her through how she might have asked a different question here or made a different suggestion there. Then we agreed on a follow-up to the customer's call."

Attention to detail and a constant search for ways to improve mark the great athlete — and the great training manager.

I told Bill it sounded like he had covered all of the bases.

"Oh, I know," he replied, "that's not the question part. The question is how long do I have to coach a person like this? When will I have her fully empowered?"

"How long has she been with you?" I asked.

"Oh, coming on 11 years," he said.

The Fine-Tuning Never Ends

Both the content and context of Bill's bemusement struck a chord with me. Here was a very capable manager, with a high-performing, loyal, and effective employee, and both were wondering whether one or the other wasn't in some way a failure — he for not being able to make the employee a fully functioning, empowered worker, and she for needing coaching on customer relations after 11 years on the job.

As I listened, it seemed to me that Bill, an avid reader of management advice books, was being led slightly astray by his desire to be the best manager possible, and was taking too literally the mandates in several best-selling business books. A fully functioning, empowered employee is not necessarily — or even desirably — an employee free of the need for feedback, counsel and, occasionally, correction.

By analogy, the best performers in the world of sports never outgrow their need for coaching. Professional tennis players like Pete Sampras, Andre Agassi, or Steffi Graff are watched over from the stands by hawk-eyed coaches, ever alert for the sudden appearance of bad habits in their games. Professional golfers on the men's and women's tours go in search of people like Harvey Penick — coach of choice to some of golf's greats for decades until his recent death — at the first sign of an unintended hook or slice developing, even years after they had established their greatness. Ben Crenshaw, for example, took a putting lesson from Penick only days before winning the Masters Tournament a few years ago.

This attention to detail, and the unabashed search for help when their games have gone a bit awry, pays off handsomely for the sporting set.

Last year, for instance, the difference in earnings between the number one and number 50 money winner on the PGA tour was over $1 million. Yet the "shot production difference" between the number one and number 50 money winners was less than one stroke per round averaged over an entire season.

Success Is in the Details

The difference between the top performers and the also-rans in every field, including business, is in the details. Those top people depend emphatically on the coaching skills of the Harvey Penicks and Bill Smiths of the world, who can, and gladly do, come to the aid of players when their games are off.

Good coaching helps first-rate performers be their best each and every time they face a tough tee, a tricky backhand shot, or an upset training customer.

And the need for good coaching, like the need for nutrition and rest, recognition, and reward, is something the best players — and trainers— never outgrow.

The truly empowered, self-directed employee is the one who, like the professional athlete, knows when he or she needs the guiding hand of the topnotch coach, if only for a moment — not the one who is convinced he or she has nothing more to learn. ■

Managing By Example: How the Power of One Wins Out in a World of Teams

The popular buzz is that managers are passé. The world of tomorrow will be run by teams. Teams will set strategies. Teams will ensure quality. Teams will solve problems. Teams will improve productivity. Managers (if they exist at all, we are lead to believe), will negotiate with stockholders, lead cheers, and make tea.

No matter how the revolution turns out, there is one managerial function that will be hard to replace with team effort and pluralistic function: the manager as role model. Individual managers are the singular embodiment of the norms, values, and behavioral rules of an organization.

That message came home to me while listening to Kenneth Macke, retired chairman of Dayton Hudson Corp., speaking to a group of retail store managers about the importance of being a positive role model for the associates on the selling floor. "I was walking through one of our stores with the store's manager last week," Macke told the assembled, "when he stopped me in mid-sentence and excused himself to wait on an obviously impatient customer. I couldn't have been prouder. Here was a manager who understood customer service and putting the customer first *in the marrow of his bones.*"

As a manager, you have more influence over the troops than you often know.

Macke's comment reminded me of Will Rogers' quip, "People learn more from observation than conversation." It also reminded me of the power of behavior modeling, and a personal incident.

Last summer, on the Fourth of July, I drew the short straw and became the designated skipper for ferrying a group of neighborhood fireworks aficionados around the lake in pursuit of the perfect tricolor rocket salute. And of course the battery in the family tugboat was two starts from being done in. So I went in search of a new battery.

The nearest open store with an available marine battery turned out to be a branch of a national chain eight miles away. I trundled the old galvanic up from the lake, loaded it into the Jeep, staggered its dead weight into the store, turned in the old, picked up a replacement, and maneuvered my way to the checkout counter.

My weighty purchase reached "Hi! I'm Debbie," the cashier just as the assistant manager also walked up. He positioned himself squarely between "Hi! I'm Debbie" and me. When Debbie tried to slip around him to wait on me, "Asst. Mgr. Ralph" raised a cautionary hand — much like an Italian traffic cop — and proceeded to instruct Debbie to "Finish this customer, close your lane, lock your cash drawer, and report to the office. Mr. Real Manager has asked me to go over your performance appraisal with you."

Debbie and I learned two important lessons that morning: First, that customers come second at Snifty-Mart. Whatever Debbie's instinct or training — and I'm told by Snifty's public relations people that all the company's Debbies go through several days of training before being loosed on customers — managers and their wishes come first. Second, that the rules of conduct, success, and longevity at Snifty aren't published in the employee handbook but rather reside in the upraised hands and whims of supervisors like "Asst. Mgr. Ralph."

Setting the Right Example

It is sometimes hard for managers to believe they have power over anyone in their organizations. Or that very much of what they say, let alone what they do, truly influences other people's behavior. But looks are deceiving.

If you are a manager and have "direct reports," it's crucial to remember those people, who invariably think of you as "the boss," are more than a little swayed by your actions. How they see you deal with and talk about peers, colleagues, employees, and customers tells them what the real rules of conduct are — no matter what your organization espouses in its vision planning, mission statement, or quality initiative.

You can't con people into doing quality work or caring about customers. But you can lead them toward that goal. Your personal example of doing things right, of taking the time to listen to customers and employees with patience, and focusing your energy on things that say "quality service" to internal clients are critical parts of your leadership role.

We asked Edward E. Crutchfield Jr., CEO and chairman of First Union Bank, how the bank went from just so-so in its perceived service quality to an acknowledged, service-superior organization. His management "secret," he says, is no secret at all. Will Rogers said it shorter, but he didn't say it any better. According to Crutchfield: "Service sinks in when managers talk and act service, service, service, day in and day out in obvious and subtle ways." ■

Quotable Quotes: Much Training Wisdom Is Packed Into a Few Well-Chosen Words

Everyone has a favorite quote or two...or three. One of my favorites, second only in my affection to Yogi Berra's infamous "It ain't over til it's over," and only slightly ahead of Mark Twain's immortal "There are three kinds of untruth in the world: Lies, damned lies and statistics!" is from the mighty pen of Joseph Conrad: *"The mind of man is capable of anything, because everything is in it, all the past, as well as the future."* A valued touchstone, this provocative pearl has, over the years and often at just the right times, reminded me of the true locus of change in the world.

A pair of HRD-related quotes I'm fond of owe their origin to Geary Rummler: "He who controls the measurement controls the results." That says a lot in a few words, as does the equally pithy, "Put a good performer into a bad system and the system wins every time."

That's the core of what makes a quotable quotation; economy, often to the point of spareness, but with hooks, a sort of intellectual Velcro that attaches itself to the inside of your head.

"Choose only to work with people who want to make things better and avoid those who want to chew on your anatomy."

All of this is, as you have undoubtedly surmised, a lead-in to a dump of my favorite overheard, begged, borrowed, pilfered and purloined training and development words of quotable wisdom.

Jay Beecroft, retired 3M training head, put the T&D role in an interesting new perspective for me when, during an interview, he allowed that "Training people don't do anything a good line manager couldn't do, if he or she had the time." And, "A training person who won't get down in the trenches and help managers turn theory into practice is a fraud."

That brings to mind a question I heard CBT consultant Sheldon Fisher put to a group of trainers at a conference when a show of hands revealed only one in four to be using any automation in their department management: "If you aren't using computers to help manage the training function, how can you possibly be encouraging other people in your organization to risk giving new ideas a chance?"

Atlanta consultant George Selin's advice about how you can figure out where to do a needs assessment also comes frequently to mind. "Find out where a line manager is getting his or her butt kicked in and help 'em get that situation reversed."

The same goes for Helene Curtis Inc. training director Matt Hennecke's response to the question, "How do you find out what training is really needed by first-line supervisors?" "If you really want to know what a supervisor is good or bad at, don't ask him, ask his employees."

Jeff Nelson, a Newport News, VA training consultant, set off some alarms with this advise on dealing with a client who wants the program "yesterday." "Every client wants it done cheap, fast and good. I tell them I can guarantee two out of three and ask, 'Which two do you want it to be?'"

The same sort of "Amen" accompanies this advice from Jim Robinson of Pittsburgh-based Partners in Change, given when he was asked how to deal with resistive clients. Said Robinson: "Don't try to save the world — or people — from themselves. The goal should be to work with people who want to make things better where they are, and to avoid those who simply want to chew on your anatomy."

Three from Bob Pike, classroom training techniques guru, have always seemed eminently reasonable. (1) "It is a law of nature that all the Magic Markers go dry at the same time." (2) "You don't have to be creative to be good, just resourceful. After all, nobody likes an expert." (3) "With any group you can count on about 90 minutes of rapt attention and about 20 minutes of real attention."

Jerome Peloguin of International Education Consultants in Philadelphia is in and of himself a memorable character. Some of his advice is equally hard to forget. Take his advice on tackling difficult projects, for instance: "If it can't be done, then don't do it!"

Dean R. Spitzer of Milwaukee is almost always equal parts curmudgeon and sage. Two of my favorites from his seemingly endless store of ideas for trainers are clearly cautionary: "Ninety percent of all training is aimed at symptoms rather than at real needs and problems." And, "Most supervisors are gutless when it comes to giving truthful performance evaluations." ∎

Take the 3 a.m. Test to Determine the Impact of Your Training Function

I had been at an ASTD conference and was feeling pretty good about myself, the world, and the importance of the things you and I do for a living. We had pontificated about the role of HRD in helping America compete in the world market, taking a serious stab at questions like, "What can trainers do to make America more competitive in the world?" which can make you feel downright important and not a little giddy.

Until the plane ride home, that is.

My seat mate was a fellow attendee — a training director from a *Fortune* 1000 insurance company and a lady of long acquaintance — who runs a tidy little training shop. She and her troops have a reputation for getting things done. If anyone could claim to be an example for others in the field, she could. Or so I would have bet.

"You get kudos from everyone who has ever worked for you or consulted with you," I said. "Do you honestly think you really make a difference in your company? That what you do makes your corporation more competitive?" Her answer was thoughtful, solid, and sobering.

There are many ways to measure your contributions, but none is more important than understanding your own motivations.

"I hope so, but I really don't know. Oh, we play all the right games. We can run the numbers with the best of them and prove that we've had an impact. But does that mean we are helping the company be competitive? I don't know. We're profitable, but how much of that is our fault and how much of it is dumb luck, I wouldn't want to have to guess. Look at the insurance-related litigation problems in this country. Look at the way rates for health care keep going up, or the cost of physician liability."

Knowing my way around this kind of angst as I do, I stepped between my friend and her obvious conclusion. "Look, you can't take that sort of perspective. That's a societal problem. What's going on in your training department that you are proud of or seems to be working in your favor?" I asked.

"We've got a good management development program," she said. "A lot of nice programs that people rave about. But I don't get involved in those things the way I used to. When you're the boss, you more often than not get the hind-end stuff to work on, the things no one else would touch.

"Last week I spent almost three days talking the senior management team into rethinking an executive development wilderness weekend. God! Their only rationale for doing it was that a competitor's senior management team had done it. At least I got them to pay for it out of the convention budget and not take the money out of my executive development pocket.

"What's frustrating is that it doesn't end. There's always another get-well-quick geek trying to get top management's ear. None of them ever seems to get around to mentioning how much work and effort it will take to make the Great Visioning come to pass. I get stuck having to explain that one.

"But the topper was a call I got from the personnel coordinator in one of our regional offices. During cutbacks a few months ago I had to lay off one of my stand-up training people. On her way out, she grabbed a copy of every program we've built or bought in the last two years and has set herself up in the consulting business.

"Wait! Wait! That's not the funny part. The funny part is that she has been out selling the productivity improvement program to our regional office people. Her pitch has been that she can do it for them cheaper and in less time than the corporate training group because she doesn't have all the politics and overhead to deal with. The killer is that we don't charge back. So they are paying $5,000 for a program that is one day shorter than the one we designed, and was theirs for free to begin with.

"So tell me, smart guy," she concluded. "Am I doing something to make my company more competitive in the world economy or am I simply standing around being nibbled to death by the ducks?"

Her point is a good one. How do we know that we are doing the right things? Or that those "right things" are making any semblance of a difference to our company?

There are statistical measures: pre/post-test, control group vs. trained group, and the like. And there are strategic plan match-up things. They all count. But there is one more indicator that I'd suggest. It's the 3 a.m. Test: It's the night before a big presentation to the executive committee. You can't sleep, and, so as not to wake anyone during the wee hours, you just have to quietly wonder and worry. What is it that you keep coming back to? Do you worry most about how you're going to come off the next day? Is it the way your staff is going to look at you if you get a turn down?

Undoubtedly it's all of that. But if it's also the thought that if you can't convince them to tackle the problem, a critical window of competitive opportunity will be missed — and, yes, some good people will continue to be frustrated — then it's a good bet your compass is working and you are headed true North. ■

How to Keep Your Job: Kiss Up — and Often

My best buddy lost her job. That's a euphemism. She wasn't walking down the street in a high wind that blew it out of her hand. She was laid off. ("Not fired," she corrects when I inadvertently use the "F" word. "Fired is when you've done something wrong. Laid off is when *they* have.") Her boss was laid off, too. So was the whole training department she was working in — save a couple of bodies the company needed to keep around for legal purposes and for show.

This was not a follow-every-fad training department. I say this despite the fact that it arranged one of those white-water rafting and team-building boondoggles for senior management back when that was fashionable. As far as I could tell, most of what the department did came straight out of the handbook: the one called "How to Run a Strategically Important HRD Function That Won't Ever Get Axed."

In the end it didn't really matter. Somebody in senior management made a bad investment decision, and when the junk-bond market collapsed, so did the company's big fat reserve. Out the window with the reserve went all interest in anything HRDish. Strategic thinking, long-term planning and acquisition proposals came off the agenda. They were replaced by cost cutting and "sell, sell, sell." Goodbye to anything or anyone who couldn't generate an immediate profit.

> *Your only true loyalties are to yourself, your family and your friends — not your company.*

What is the concerned HRD type to do? Journalist Jane Ciabattari has assembled some good survival advice in her book, *Winning Moves: How To Come Out Ahead in a Corporate Shake-Up.* Parts of her counsel have to do with revising assumptions and feelings about work:

■ *Understand that job security is an antiquated concept.* Forget the quaint idea that hard work and sacrifice are always rewarded. You aren't your job, and your job isn't your life. Your only legitimate loyalties are to yourself, your family and your friends. Circle the wagons there, not around pie-in-the-sky promises from an employer.

■ *Understand that you don't "own" your job.* But you do own your skills, training and experience, which are highly portable. If you haven't been keeping in touch with the local labor market, old bosses and ex-coworkers, taking occasional interviews and the like, start making up lost ground — now.

■ *Understand that you will end up with a different job, whether you go or stay.* A new team or just a new business strategy will have an impact on what you do day-to-day, as well as on your future prospects. It doesn't matter whether your company is acquired, merged, downsized or just reorganized — things will never be the same. At the very least, be ready to "reevaluate" the situation.

Find Ciabattari's advice a little too reactive and passive? You might be interested in an alternative strategy I recently stumbled over in *Fortune* magazine. Seems that a professor of psychology at Bryant College in Rhode Island, one Donald Deluga, has found a high correlation between organizational success and what he refers to as "ingratiation." What he means is basic brownnosing. There are three major ways to go at it:

■ *Flattery.* Figure out who talks to your boss on a regular basis: a secretary, a coworker who loves to snitch and tell, even your boss's boss will do. Say something good about your boss to or in front of that person. Mutter something about what an honor it is to work for "someone like Mr. Dithers — so wise and so respected in the industry." Rest assured it will be passed along.

■ *Opinion conformity.* Intentionally disagree with your boss, only to yield gracefully later. Bosses apparently feel good if they can persuade you to change your mind. For good measure, throw yourself on your knees and cry, "Gosh, Mr. Dithers, I don't know why I even bother to disagree with you. You always seem to have your finger on the pulse of the industry."

■ *Self-preservation.* Present yourself as what you perceive is your boss's idea of a perfect employee. Self-deprecation works well for some, says Deluga. His theory is that admission of a weakness by an employee establishes a bond of trust. You might, for instance, try, "Gee, Mr. Dithers, I wish I could handle those three-toed sloths from accounting the way you do."

Naw...better to get laid off, and be able to look yourself in the mirror in the morning. ■

Why Protecting Your Oddball Employees Is Good Business

A few days before Christmas my wife and I were in New Haven, CT, home to Yale University and the Yale Repertory Theater. We were there for a performance of a visiting repertory company Susan does volunteer work for in Minneapolis. On a Sunday morning we hiked the Yale campus in search of a greasy-spoon breakfast. The tiny, cracked-tile grill we wandered into was the real McCoy — right down to the eccentric customer in a side booth simultaneously smoking three cigarettes and arguing aloud with *The New York Times* editorial page. But far from being a distraction or disruption, this energetic eccentric gave the misty gray morning a sense of purpose and energy. And it all reminded me of how flat and spiceless organizational life can be when it is purposely stripped of characters and eccentrics.

Eccentrics ask the kinds of questions that jog companies from a 'business as usual' stupor.

Pop psych guru Wayne Dyer, author of *Your Erroneous Zones* and several other "you can do it if you try" books, calls the characters among us Scurvy Elephants; a malapropism held over from his childhood when he misheard one teacher describe him to another as a "disruptive element."

He was to later preach that it was perhaps the finest unintended compliment he was ever to receive.

More years ago than I care to count, I heard a personnel researcher from IBM explain how she and her colleagues had spent years learning to scientifically sort the best and brightest students from the world's top universities into two piles: IBM material and "other." Toward the end of her presentation she said, "Of course the end result of our work is that we are now able to regularly and reliably hire people just like the people who already work here. But I am not necessarily convinced that is the wisest course." Her concern was for the unthinking sameness of minds too alike to challenge the obvious — for the determined exclusion of Scurvy Elephants.

Protecting Endangered Elephants

Sitting there in that breakfast bistro, I couldn't help wondering just how many organizations are this day using the challenges of cost containment or productivity improvement to purge the Scurvy Elephants who have slipped onto their payrolls. My fear is the number is uncomfortably large. Worse is the message such ousters send. The oft-heard Japanese axiom about the "nail that sticks up being the first pounded down" is as apt in the West as it is in the East.

It seems to me we are in a day and time when the Scurvy Elephants of the world should be looked upon as a scarce resource in need of preservation and careful nurturing, rather than as nuisances in need of purging. For all the Hosannas about total quality, reengineering and teamwork, it is still the eccentric, oddball character who routinely and often maddeningly sees the world through important "other" eyes. It is the Scurvy Elephant who has the audacity — or naivete — to ask those irritatingly dumb questions like, "Hey, why do we park in the driveway, and drive on the parkway?" Or simply, "But why can't we get back to customers within 24 hours?" Questions that need to be asked often and routinely to jog us from the stupor of our set ways and challenge us to stop talking about change and actually bring some to pass.

Needed: VP in Charge of Eccentric Employees

Toward that end, I propose every organization embarking on a major reorganizing campaign establish an Office of Scurvy Elephants, or, at the very least, appoint a Vice President in Charge of Scurvy Elephants. That noble office or officer would be charged with ensuring that every quality or service-related task force includes a resident eccentric with a track record of meeting disruption, a history of "side-ways" thinking and a poor attention span. If the number of natural SEs in your organization is insufficient, the VP of SEs could appoint temporary SEs. A temporary SE could wear a ball cap or T-shirt with "Scurvy Elephant of the Day" emblazoned on it. If that isn't subtle enough for your culture, the badge, shirt, or hat might simply read "Temporary Disruptive Force."

This may be a hard concept to sell to your organization. So I suggest that rather than publishing a Scurvy Elephant Position Paper or bringing in a high-priced Scurvy Elephant consultant, you subtly insinuate the idea into your culture by modeling it in your department. For instance, in every future customer service or reengineering workshop conducted under your banner, one attendee can be designated the Customer Spokesperson or Scurvy Elephant, given a hat, badge, or shirt and instructed to raise customer issues and generally speak up for the customer at every opportunity throughout the workshop. This will of course raise havoc with your instructors' nerves and other attendees' ability to doze off during class, but that's the point, isn't it? To disrupt, challenge and cause creative irritation.

Think of embracing the Scurvy Elephant ethic as a diversity tool. After all, diversity of viewpoint and heterogeneity of ideas may, ultimately, be the zenith of all diversity aspirations. ∎

Collar Wars: Those Who Wear the White Might Be Giving Others the Blues

The Saturday before Christmas our dishwasher broke. We had filled it to the brim with the week's nastiness, shut the door, and pushed the cycle selector button. For about 30 seconds, everything was a go. But then Mr. Whirlpool's miracle machine sputtered like a '56 Desoto on a cold morning, sloshed, groaned twice, and died.

Three door slams later, it was obvious we were in trouble. Nothing in the manufacturer's *Problem Solving For Complete Idiots* booklet helped. Outside expertise was definitely called for.

Ten people were due for dinner Christmas Day, and most of our usable "fit for company" dishes were hardening in the muck and mire of an unfinished heavy load cycle. We were 10 hours of cooking and three dishwasher loads of pots and pans away from being ready. Our calls to repair people were futile.

Then luck struck. Karl at the hardware store knew a guy named Al who had bought his cousin Ole's appliance repair business, and Al knew Whirlpool real good.

At the heart of good performance is pride, which we may unwittingly be undermining.

Although Al was booked up, he knew this guy Dave who worked out of his house, had a beeper, and liked to make house calls. Dave was at our place in less than an hour.

It gets better. Dave was an affable young whiz. He quickly spotted the problem: "Yep. She's the door switch all right. Thought it might be that from the way ya described 'er over the phone." And of course, Dave had picked up a door switch just in case he was right in his over-the-phone diagnosis. "Shouldn't take more'n 20 minutes." He was done in 13.

Over coffee we learned Dave was a college dropout. "I shoulda gone back and got a real education, but I was pretty hot for gettin' a job and married and all. And then of course I got drafted and so on and here I am, just fixin' washin' machines." Which to my way of thinking at the moment was but a short distance from being a practicing Nobel Laureate in physics.

So what would Dave rather be doing? Well, actually, he enjoys the work, earns good money, and likes being his own boss.

So what was his big regret about college?

"Well I don't know, but maybe I coulda been more. Maybe had an office job or something."

I was perplexed. "Let me get this straight. You like your work. You own your own business. You're doing well. You're thinking about expanding. And you wonder if you wouldn't be better off sitting on your butt all day, shuffling papers and going to meetings?"

"Well, no. I don't know. Maybe not when you put it that way…"

Blue-Collar Blues

And I don't know either. I don't know when or how white-shirt office work became more important and more valued than blue-collar work. And I don't know how wearing a tie and worrying about who has the biggest desk or the most sub-toadies became a "career," and building products and performing services for customers became "just a job."

A few weeks ago the quality guru of a large industrial company was giving me a rundown of his group's accomplishments. In one of his scrapbooks were photographs of a small group of miners, a mile underground, meeting to discuss productivity, quality, and the like. "They've made more improvements in productivity and safety in the past 18 months than the so-called professionals have in the last 10 years," he marveled.

Exaggeration? Maybe. But through my friend's prideful answer glowed a hint to unraveling my "Dave dilemma." The siren call of Professionalism — to be someone with a degree, and certification, and accreditation. To be someone with a right to an opinion beyond the mundane.

As a sarcastic friend puts it: "Use all the fancy language you want, but there are only three kinds of work: moving things close to the face of the earth, supervising those who move things close to the face of the earth, and engineering. And nobody knows exactly what engineers do."

Dave isn't sure what he is, but he suspects he's "just labor," and suspects that isn't good. You and I don't discourage his thinking. After all, we aren't exactly sure what we are.

When was the last time you thought to yourself, after watching the Daves of the world: "Thank God I don't have to do that to make a living!" But then try on this question: "Is it just possible that I might, albeit inadvertently, be one of the reasons there are Daves in my world who fix things and make things and do the thousand and one important jobs that go together to make an enterprise click — but who don't see what they do as important enough to take pride in?"

Are we really looking for solutions, or are we just another part of the problem? ■

Handling Vendors:
Setting Guidelines Can Help
You Control Pesky Salespeople

A strange call. Particularly strange for a Sunday afternoon. "Ron, my name is Smeed Bumbly (not his real name, but his real behavior). I want to talk to you about...*The Communications Course.*" You could tell from the two-beat pause after "about" and the hushed way he said The Communications Course that we were dealing with a True Believer.

"Where did you get my name and why are you calling me at home on a Sunday afternoon?"

"Well. I, er, got your name from David Duck-This-One-Fast at MCorp. I was explaining *The Course* to him, and how it had changed my life, and how important it is that he put everyone at MCorp through it when he mentioned you. He told me he would consider sending people to *The Course* about the same time Ron Zemke became a graduate. So I'm calling to see when you'd like to attend. But to tell the truth, I'm puzzled. Could you tell me who you are, and why someone at MCorp would care about your opinion of *The Course?*"

> *Your time is valuable. Don't waste it listening to pitches for products you don't need.*

What followed was not pretty — not for a Sunday afternoon, not even for a Friday night in Times Square.

Later, reflecting on the peculiarity of the incident, I recalled a complaint I had heard and dismissed several times in the last few months. As one exasperated training director put it, "As if my plate isn't full enough, with cutbacks and task forces and hiring freezes — the vendors are turning strange on me! They used to want to sell me things. Now they want to 'dialogue about my needs' and 'discuss ways of strengthening our relationship.' I hardly have time to strengthen my relationship with my kids, let alone some salesperson who wants to waste my day with some getting-to-know-me-and-my-company-better drivel!"

To tell you the truth, I haven't much sympathy for the complaint. It's not that I'm enamored with vendor reps who think nothing of wasting a client's time with learning-about-your-company lessons. I am just more tolerant of salespeople and their sometimes peculiar antics than I am of training executives who can't or won't set them straight when need be.

Sales reps have one job, to sell. That they sometimes hide that intent behind such silly shrubbery as "mutually exploring ways to better meet your needs" doesn't invalidate the possibility that what they sell may be of value, or that they might be of some help in meeting needs of your organization.

But salespeople have to be managed if they are going to be a help. Unmanaged, they start managing you, arranging your time and setting your priorities. They see their time as valuable too, and will act to maximize theirs if they don't perceive you needing to be efficient with yours.

Intrigued, I interviewed my favorite training director — the one I live with. Her best advice, leavened with a couple of ideas I've gleaned from others: Be clear, be careful, and be courteous — up to a threshold.

1. Decide how and when you want to see vendors. Do you want to batch sales calls? Only see salespeople on certain days of the month? You must make that policy clear to salespeople when they call looking for "just a few minutes of your time while they are in town."

2. Pre-screen appointments. Most of the things people want to pitch to you are probably of marginal current value. Note the word current. Most training execs hate to say no to salespeople because they're sure that as soon as they blow off the "File Cabinet Strategies and You" program, somebody is going to ask for it. Instead of deciding yes or no on a cold call, ask the vendor to send materials, promise a telephone follow-up scheduled at your convenience, and only acquiesce to a face-to-face if those screens show something promising.

3. Discourage chats. Once you realize phrases like, "Get together to discuss your needs" are tactics to get you to agree to a sales call, you won't feel bad about rejecting such offers in favor of focused, objectives-on-the-table sales calls.

4. Define the time line. A sales call only has to last as long as you want. If you think that a preliminary call should last 30 minutes, schedule 30 minutes. The rep who insists, "You need a full day with me to appreciate the difference between our course and everything else ever offered in the history of Western civilization," has the problem, not you.

5. Disallow walk-ins. The age of the old canvas is gone; it isn't profitable for anyone. Even if you aren't busy when a cold caller comes by, don't visit. Explain you don't accept cold calls. Accept any proffered literature, and be done with it.

6. Don't buy into intimidation tactics. Some salespeople, when rebuffed, go into the old I-happen-to-know-your-chairman-is-very-interested-in-this routine. OK, so the jerk can read an annual report. And maybe he — it tends to be male reps putting this move on females — has sent a note or a brochure to someone above you in the corporate pecking order. Big deal: (A) If the Mr./Ms. Big being referred to wanted you to see this person, you'd already know about it. (B) If you are likely to get in trouble for making a salesperson act like a salesperson, it's a dumb place to work in the first place. Besides, you can always apologize later. We know of a vendor who threatened to take his money out of a trainer's employing bank if not granted an interview. The branch manager was upset. The CEO just laughed himself silly. ∎

Beware the Training Offer that Comes with a 'Scientifically Proven' Label

The revival of an old wheeze caught my eye while reading a training technology journal recently. The writers, a couple of well-meaning consultants, ended their explanation of "The Systems Approach to Training" with the promise that by following the dictates of this scientific approach, the reader would be able to produce better training than by.... They never did specify what their recommended approach was "better" than; it was just better. Maybe "better than anything else they could possibly imagine" was the intended object of their verbiage. It certainly was the intent of their article.

What struck me was the easily discerned assumption that the particular assemblage of prescriptions, boxes, and arrows the authors used was *the one and only* "scientific" approach to developing and delivering training. My second reaction, which came a few weeks later, was different. This time, thanks to an article entitled "Scientific and Unscientific Approaches to Quality Improvement" — an article dedicated to proving that the only scientific approach to TQM is statistical process control — I began to wonder just what the heck a "scientific approach" to anything should mean.

If the proof is in the pudding, then most 'scientific' claims are very hard on the palate.

Ask Mr. Wizard

I do know what a toothpaste advertiser is trying to claim when someone in the advertising department decides to write an ad using phrases like "scientifically proven to whiten and brighten your teeth." And I know, in general, what it means to say that something was developed through years of scientific research in the laboratories of Snicklefritz University. But what precisely does it mean when some training or quality guru claims: "This here is the best way to do things because it is the 'scientific' way?"

A trip to Webster's New Collegiate wasn't all that helpful. But like saying grace over a greasy spoon meal, it didn't hurt anything, either. Science, Webster's says, is "the observation, identification, description, experimental investigation, and theoretical explanation of natural phenomena." This suggests that the university professor who has made the study of nude beaches his specialty could, contrary to the opinion of the committee that denied him tenure, indeed be practicing science.

How about the "scientific method?" Webster's defines it as "the principles or processes regarded as characteristic of or needed for scientific investigation, including rules for forming concepts, conduct of observations and experiments, and validation of hypothesis by observation or experiment." So if by scientific these authors mean experimental, then what they should be offering us is a controlled study of various methods to see which actually works best in our organizations, right? But how often do you see that done? And would your management go for such a process if it were proposed?

Perhaps what they mean by scientific is the "Ask Mr. Wizard" junior high school approach to science: observable cause and effect. Seal the mouse in a plastic bottle overnight and it will die, which proves that mice are allergic to plastic bottles.

Larry Bird: Trainer Nonpareil

But that form of science doesn't hold up well under the "Larry Bird" test. When asked how to become a superstar basketball player, Mr. Bird, a former Boston Celtic, advised a group of starry-eyed youthful fans that his secret was practice, practice, practice. "As a boy growing up in Indiana I shot hundreds if not thousands of practice shots in my backyard day in and day out," he said. The problem, of course, is that this advice doesn't account for successful superstars who *don't* spend day and night shooting jump shots and free throws in the driveway, or for the unsuccessful Michael Jordan wanna-bes who do.

I'm afraid that for too many of these authors the science in their scientific approach is something more akin to Mary Baker Eddy's use of the word science — as in Christian Science: "A belief in healing through prayer." Do exactly what we tell you to do, believe exactly what we tell you to believe, pray a lot, and you will get to training or total quality heaven.

Sorry, but that for me, as Hamlet said to Horatio, excludes too many things in heaven and Earth; too many possibilities.

So the next time some vendor claims that what he or she is about to ask you to buy is absolutely scientifically proven, it would be a good idea to lock up your cash drawer and start asking for a little "scientific" proof of that claim. ■

Malfeasance in Feedback: Are We Taking the Humanity Out of HRD?

The guy in the next airline seat over was youngish, yuppish, and obviously agitated. Twice he pulled from his satchel a large, flat, white envelope, removed and read the contents, grimaced, returned the contents to the envelope, put the envelope back in the briefcase, and restowed the case under the seat in front of him.

Cycle three turned my mild interest to genuine curiosity. So, a slight twist in my seat easily brought into focus the object of consternation: six typed pages headed, "YOUR LEADERSHIP STYLE." It wasn't too hard to figure out exactly what it was about the contents of those six pages that had my flight mate so upset, since he had circled and repeatedly underscored several passages. Who wouldn't have a question or two about something subtitled, "A Personal and Confidential Feedback Report" containing phrases like "...is self-confident to the point of arrogance and rigidity...," "...tends to be extremely demanding of subordinates...," and "...will frequently ignore the feelings of others in pursuit of bottom-line results?"

I learned, while chatting over what the airline was passing off as food, that Paul was going to a four-day sales management seminar conducted at his company's home office by an outside consulting organization. The feedback report he was so upset about, it turns out, was the result of a survey he had hastily filled out and sent back to the consulting company the week before. As we talked, his consternation seemed to grow. "My God!" he exclaimed at one point, "I'm not even sure I really read the damn thing when I filled it out. I just hope they haven't shown it around the division. My boss's boss is one of those real people-oriented types. If he decides I'm insensitive to people or not a team player or something, I could be washed up."

> *It's arrogant to think we can reduce an individual into a neat package, which can then be summarized in a few hundred words.*

Having more than a little empathy for Paul's upset, I tried oiling the waters with a couple of soothing remarks about taking those things with a grain of salt, and that, in the last analysis, he himself was the final arbiter. It was up to him to decide if the analysis was valid. Besides, any ethical consultant would undoubtedly hold the results in confidence.

I hope he was reassured. I hope he was confident that no one was going to end his career over the results of a very general and possibly suspect survey, and that the results shouldn't be construed as implying that he has some great personality or character flaw, some mark of Cain. I hope he was reassured that his company, and the consulting group they had engaged for this training, were interested in his growth and development and not looking for an excuse to eliminate him from the career-progression stream.

For my part, I was not confident or reassured. I was, in fact, just plain outraged.

I'm not completely sure what set me off. At first blush, I assumed it was simply the arrogance I sometimes see lurking implicitly in the act of purporting to be able to sum up an individual in six bedeviling pages of print and a handful of graphic squiggles. (If the truth be known, I haven't been comfortable with these kinds of tests since a high school guidance counselor decided my profile on an interest test proved I would do well to forget about college and think about carrying on the family trade: laboring in the steel mills.)

But paranoia passes, and on further reflection I see a sort of abject carelessness at the core of what had ticked me off. It was, and is, my astonishment at the thoughtless and cavalier behavior of the consultants involved. How dare he/she/they dump such a heavy bucket of normative conjecture and raw presumption on a person without so much as a mitigating warning, some simple, honest declaration that the results of the profile report were based on broad norms and might not be applicable in every case? How could someone in our business have become so callous and unfeeling, so drained of simple human warmth, as to unceremoniously inflict so sensitive and potentially so hurtful a message on another individual through the mail?

When Shakespeare's Mark Antony observed that "The fault lies not in our stars but within ourselves that we are underlings," it was a message aimed at us all, test makers and test takers alike. In the final analysis, my question is simply this: Have some of us become so successful at making a business of what we do that we have lost the sense of simple humanity implicit in the phrase "human resource development"? ∎

Socratic Training: Would You Ever Really Use This Poisonous Approach?

A little learning is a dangerous thing — or so conjectured Alexander Pope in 1711 in an essay on the art of criticism:

> A little learning is a dangerous thing,
> Drink deep or taste not the Perian spring,
> There shallow draughts intoxicate the brain,
> And drinking largely sobers us again.

We have, for better or worse, conspired to immortalize just one line of that stanza. Unlike so many oft garbled famous sayings, this piece of doggerel loses little in either abbreviation or translation. That singular distinction came to mind the other day as I played observer to a young consultant doing a train-the-trainer session for a mutual client. I was astonished — that's polite for I couldn't believe my ears — as Junior admonished, his index finger wagging, this gaggle of part-time trainers-to-be not to lecture their trainees, but to "engage them in a Socratic dialogue." Our facile facilitator explained: "The Greek philosopher Socrates is considered one of the best teachers who ever lived. From him we learn that a good trainer asks frequent and challenging questions so as to keep students engaged with the material."

Lesson #1 in Socrates' classroom: Don't get called on. Lesson #2: Don't challenge the old guy's answers.

Apparently the closest this trainer had come to engaging that crusty old antideist was the movie *Bill and Ted's Excellent Adventure* (Fox, 1989). As I remember Plato's painfully detailed descriptions of Socrates' approach to "instructing" others, the hemlock was letting Socrates off easy.

A quick review from Western Civilization 101: Socrates lived sometime around 400 BC. What we know of him is second hand from one of his students, Plato, who wrote a book called *The Dialogues*, which purports to recount Socrates' teachings as well as his technique. Apparently Socrates thought pretty highly of himself. He confided to Plato, "I am the wisest of all people, because I know so little." He would have made a great vice president of HR.

According to Plato, Socrates died because he was just too smart for his own good. The elders of Athens tried and convicted Socrates for preaching against the gods — always a big mistake in a town where the highest point of land is occupied by a church — and for corrupting the youth of the Athenian city-state. He was condemned to the aforementioned poisonous sangria mix.

Making of a Legend

Once Socrates was safely dead, Plato set out to make him a legend. From Plato's perspective, Socrates was a great teacher, a fantastic performer whose lessons were full of verbal pyrotechnics and humor. The recounting of his interactive lectures made for great copy — and an easy lesson plan for the ensuing 20 or so generations of philosophy and law professors.

But to really understand Socrates as a teacher, don't look at his clever questions and his Roman-candle conclusions. Study instead the student's side of any of the dialogues and you'll see the point. In one, Socrates pins a kid named Meno against the wall. It's a great logical rollercoaster ride — unless you look at the kid's side of the discussion:

MENO: "Yes, Socrates."
MENO: "No, Socrates."
MENO: "I believe so, Socrates."
MENO: "I don't think so Socrates."
MENO: "I'm getting a migraine Socrates."
MENO: "You're amazing, Socrates! Flippin' amazing!"

What Socrates' students most clearly learned was: (1) Try not to get called on, no matter what this old dude asks, because it's always a trick question, and (2) When it's your turn in the barrel, keep your head down and play the straight man. This is not simply my opinion on the matter. The professional Greekologists have even given a special name to Socrates' cute little teaching technique. They call it "Socratic Irony," meaning acting dumb to show how smart you really are.

Socrates probably lifted the idea from Greek theater, where every play had a mandatory character called the "eiron." The eiron's role was to walk about and, by asking seemingly dumb questions, expose the ludicrous nature of the thoughts and actions of others, especially the terminally pompous and morally flawed. The eiron's purpose was not to enlighten or transform the questionee, but to entertain those who were in on the game — the audience.

If you have an audience to entertain and a biographer to keep busy, The Socratic Method has a lot of merit. If you are more interested in creating a safe haven for a fair exchange of ideas and issues, you might want to look someplace else for a role model for your new trainers. ■

Teaching Managers to Do Everything Means They Won't Master Anything

Management — the concept — is dead.

That, at least, is the strongly held view of Robert J. Samuelson, economist, MIT professor, and regular columnist for *Newsweek*. In a column in that magazine, Samuelson attributes the temporary collapse of Sears, Westinghouse, and IBM to that popular American business school ideal and training aim: the perpetuation of the jack-of-all-trades "general" manager, and the accompanying belief that a well-trained manager can manage virtually anything…and succeed at it.

Writes Samuelson:

"With hindsight, we can see the absurdity. We don't imagine a winning football coach switching to basketball, nor a concert pianist becoming a symphony violinist. We don't think an orthopedic surgeon would automatically make a good psychiatrist. We recognize that differences in talent, temperament, knowledge, and experience make some people good at some things and not at others. Somehow, managers are supposed to be immune to this logic."

Samuelson is not the only pundit who sees a problem with the proposition that "a manager is a manager is a manager." McGill University professor Henry Mintzberg recently criticized the concept of the MBA degree as "not very useful" and as serving only to create graduates who are "glib and quick-witted" and committed primarily to their own personal advancement.

Management skills aren't easily transferable — and too many training directors are slow to recognize it.

Samuelson criticizes the Harvard Business School for, in effect, creating a credential that has become primarily a union card and passport to the ranks of overpaid, know-little, puff-a-lots. His heroes, the exemplars of real managerial skill, are the Sam Walton, Ray Kroc, and Bill Gates types who he describes as "semi-fanatics who doggedly pursued a few good ideas."

Samuelson doesn't say much about the exorbitant dollars that are routinely showered on those failed general managers, or how those same said dollars drive good technical specialists into the ranks of those aspiring to become mediocre, overpaid, and pampered generalists.

The Trappings of 'Corporate Universities'

Mulling over Samuelson's critique brought to mind several thoughts. One was a re-evaluation of a common trend of the last few decades: the drive to legitimize training and development through the development of a "Corporate University." The idea of a training department taking on airs, creating complex competency maps, publishing catalogs of coded curricula — "Marketing 103: Aimed at level D4 and D5 product manager positions, focusing on marketing competencies C-1-Z, B-6-T" — has always tickled me.

What had not occurred to me until I read Samuelson's castigations is that in addition to wasting resources, such pretensions might also be harmful to the long-term health of the businesses they're purporting to serve.

Consider: If the purpose of a staff department such as training is to aid in accomplishing a marketplace mission, just how helpful to that end is the pursuit of ideas (training line managers to be generalists) that Samuelson is so clearly pointing to as counterproductive to organizational survival?

Truth be known, most training executives might say they're not all that committed to their organizations anyway. One more hiccup in the widget market, they surmise, and they'll be the next ones taking residency in Pink Slip Land. I suspect training execs' real turn-on is still the development of human potential; helping people become all that they can be. To that, I say "wonderful." But I also ask: How big a favor are you doing employees by focusing their attention not on skills for surviving the uncertain '90s, but on the troublesome idea that a manager is a manager is a manager, that technical skills are for technicians and doing actual value-adding work is a dated approach?

The real point for me in Samuelson's complaint isn't that managing shouldn't be considered an important and trainable skill, or that management isn't a legitimate form of work. The real point is that generic management skills are, while necessary, not sufficient to carry either an individual or a corporation very far in our brave new corporate world.

If we aren't training today's managers to be a part of the process of creating and delivering a marketplace advantage, what value do we add to the organization — and how do we justify our existence during the inevitable next belt-tightening? ■

CHAPTER 3

THE OFTEN-STRANGE FASCINATIONS OF HRD FOLK

INTRODUCTION

That Was Zen and This Is Now

In the spring of 1975, Marty Wong and I borrowed his housemate's wheels and tooled down to Lincoln, NE, from Minneapolis to attend what a brochure promised would be one of the "biggest blowouts ever" of the human potential movement. All the biggies — the super gurus — would be right there, live and in person, in the main ballroom of the Cornhusker Hotel: Will Schutz, Karl Pribram, George Leonard, Al Houng, Werner Erhard, and two or three of the day's best-known massage and body alignment experts.

It was obvious to anyone with the slightest trend-riding aspirations that "be there or be square" was the operative phrase.

Owing to a flat tire in Des Moines, we barely beat the opening "Ohmm" of the conference. But we scooted in just in time to be awed by the sight of 800 fellow seekers attending to Schutz's greeting: "Pull up a piece of floor and we'll begin our odyssey." For the next two days and nights we were awash in a sea of trust walks, triad dialoguing, spinal massages and Tai Chi dancing. We were regaled with Sufi wit and wisdom, challenged to touch the spiritual in ourselves, encouraged to see the connectedness of all things and lectured on using the creative sides of our brains. We shared our most intimate insecurities with perfect strangers, challenged our paradigms, got real with our feelings, and went home feeling we had indeed been transformed to another level of existence. Sort of.

Laying aside any reservations we may have felt about the lasting impact of this experience on our lives, it certainly had been a kick. We had seen the living legends of the day in action, and at the very least, we had taken yet another important step in the "becoming" journey.

And everyone we worked with thought we were speaking in tongues for the next week.

An Ephemeral Impact

Eventually, though, like a sailor back on duty after a rip-snorting shore leave, I got back to the mundaneness of making a living, writing a thesis proposal, and worrying about the crabgrass in my yard. Over the next few years there were other such shore leaves, other indulgences in other certifiably meaningful "growth" experiences through my affiliation with the HRD world: transcendental meditation, EST, relaxation response, guided imagery, rebirthing, flotation tanks, brain-training, hot-tub encounter sessions and "clearing" — the entire holistic hodgepodge.

After a while, the sparkle and allure began to fade from the prospect of another marathon cosmic-consciousness seminar, another weekend encounter with my true self. Eventually, it was impossible to deny that a pattern of predictable sameness had settled over these experiences. I shaved, cut my hair, slipped back into the straight world in a fairly straight job, and gradually lost touch with the human potential movement, with its lofty promises and peculiar avenues to truth, freedom, beauty and enlightenment.

The "Bottom-Line" '90s

For most of us in corporate HRD, that was Zen and this is now — it's a harder-edged, bottom-line-first, no-nonsense time. Those days and experiences, the vocabulary, the look and the focus, are momentos in the attic like Earth shoes and love beads. Making big bucks, searching for the latest and greatest ROI model, and figuring out how to leverage-finance a second home on two already overextended paychecks — these things take precedence over a spiritually fulfilling or philosophically consistent lifestyle.

But every once in a while, usually on a quiet autumn Friday near twilight, if I squeeze my eyes almost but-not-quite closed and look off to that peripheral spot where nothing is quite in focus, I can see the shadows Sufi dancing around the edges of the page, or in a corner of the room. And then I remember that "Is this all there is?" is only one option, and that mirth and merriment are an alternative to the dourness and solemnity with which I — dare I say we? — approach the performance enhancement work I do.

The human potential movement was, in many ways, a "Woo-Woo" world of angels dancing on pin heads. But there was within it as well a joy for having a hand in helping somebody learn to do something better, see something differently or think a thought they've never reveled in before. Beyond the urgency and serious organizational purposes, ours is still a world that dotes on new possibilities, celebrates change, and takes pleasure in the unique and different. And the world around us is sometimes a very odd place. Sometimes that peculiarity comes from the strange way we squint at that world — and sometimes it's because we are the peculiar part, all by ourselves. — **R.Z.**

Am I Self-Actualized
Or Am I a Grape?

In the great fruit salad of life, I am, it seems, an Apple-Orange. I would have thought a persimmon, had I thought about it at all, or even an avocado — at least the shape would be right. But no. According to the personality test in the variety section of the newspaper I was reading between planes in Cincinnati, I am an Apple with an Orange rising — or the other way around, depending, I suppose, on the pH of my mood.

Jane Firbank, the British clinical psychologist who made up the test, has decided that as an Apple-Orange, I approach life with drive, power and leadership desire; that's the Apple part. But I am also big on being hard-to-get-to, even-tempered and fact-oriented; that's where the Orange comes in. In any case, I am *not* a Banana — too bland and conciliatory. Nor am I a Grape — too sensual and satin-sheet-oriented for my type.

That, at least, is my interpretation of Firbank's analysis of my personality, based on the 20 questions ("You have a high sex drive: ___ True ___ False") that appeared in this particular newspaper. This harvest of 10 years of painstaking research pairs a person's favorite fruit with the core of his or her personality. It's all based on that well-known psychophysical principle, You Are What You Eat, in which case I am a cheeseburger and fries, and not a fruitcake at all.

We are destined to revere the obscure, the obtuse, the Delphic.

"Give a kid a computer and anything can be correlated," I thought smugly to myself, recalling the insight of a buddy who once helped me squeak through six miserable, mandatory graduate-school statistics courses. Late one night in the computer lab, he buoyed my flagging spirits with the whispered wisdom that my thesis would produce positive results because of an axiom about the nature of statistics: "You can prove just about anything if you can steal enough computer time."

On reflection, however, I believe I may have done the good doctor and her anthropomorphic orchard a disservice. I now suspect that she is tuned into a devastatingly simple yet profound truth. We — you and I — are forever destined to revere the obtuse, the obscure, the Delphic, and to look down our noses at the straightforward, the linear and the simple. We can't help ourselves. Faced with a choice of a tree as a potential coffee table or a tree as a symbol for the interdependence of the family of man, we pick the symbol, no contest.

The hidden meaning is the thing. A good cigar, said Freud, is more than a smoke, and a generation of novelists beat us half to death with the connec-

tive possibilities. In the Big Sur '60s and '70s, it got even more personal and we became one with our world of symbols. We were thrilled to pieces by the Swami who held his foot while chanting, "I am that, and I am that, and I am that." (Toe fungi not even considered, it seems.) And who can forget clarifying his values by contemplating such earth-shattering questions as, "Are you a mountain person or a valley person? Decide which you are and say why." I get giddy just thinking about it.

The point is that attempting to be too logical, rational and straightforward in search of personal truth may be self-defeating. Why teach someone to make a coffee table if you can baffle him with a good enigma instead? What counts is the mystery and possibility of hidden meaning in the message, not the message itself. Half the White House press corps would be out of work if we, the people, were interested in what the president or some other politician actually said, rather than what somebody else thinks he probably meant by what he said. And think back to the last department meeting you attended. What did you do afterward? Did you and your confidants sneak off to discuss what the boss said, or was the conversation really about what you thought she meant, implied, avoided or insinuated?

Next time you're looking for a training film on performance evaluation, a book on supervision, a feedback instrument or a consultant to wow the troops, shuck off that pedestrian urge to find the easiest to understand. Go for the obscure, obtuse and vague. You may not know what they learned from it. They may not know either. But they'll love you for the meaningfulness of the experience. ■

Raiders of the Lost Team-Building Metaphor

"**O**kay, team, it's time to serve up an ace, punch the old pigskin over the goal line, slap that puck right into the net! Score this one, people, and it's the Stanley Cup of sales, the World Series of marketing, the Super Bowl of R&D! Now get out there and win one for good old Acme Widget!"

No doubt about it, the sports idiom is one constant in the informal, ever-changing, often bumptious, always trendy American business lexicon. And while sports metaphors may not be everyone's cup of Gatorade, they do add a touch of color to an otherwise bloodless argot.

Trouble is, even for an audience that appreciates the attempt, jock metaphors, like any metaphors, have their limits. Blow the bubble gum too hard and it explodes. In some ways, selling life insurance is indeed like playing baseball, but in a thousand ways it isn't. Most of us, I think, understand that. We may see some informal team-building value in the sandlot ball game our salespeople play on a summer afternoon, but we don't pretend that the experience of hitting a home run will somehow transfigure Shirley, turning her from a pedestrian insurance agent into a corporate superstar.

> *It's hard to imagine the envelope of metaphorical utility being stretched more thinly.*

Sometimes, though, we do move beyond metaphorical descriptions and into the full-fledged pursuit of metaphorical excellence. That's when we start to lose our grip.

Wall Street Journal reporter Ken Wells drew an insightful parallel between the passion for jock-talk and the current team-building craze I've come to think of under the heading "managers in the woods." Nowhere, for my money, is the envelope of metaphorical utility being stretched more thinly.

All across the country, executives from such seemingly sensible companies as AT&T, Pacific Gas & Electric, Federal Express and the American Stock Exchange are being herded up mountains, hurled down raging rapids and shoved shivering out onto the frigid tundra in the name of management development. By one estimate, this year as many as 20,000 American managers will climb ropes, paddle rubber rafts and swing from tree to tree, Tarzan style, all in the expectation of achieving group cohesiveness and team synergy that will work wonders back at the office.

The line of reasoning? By attacking challenging and unfamiliar situations together, these weekend warriors will learn more about one another's strengths and weaknesses. They'll recognize the need to cooperate rather than compete (with their own team members, that is) in order to survive and thrive — in the woods, in the factory, in life.

Proof? When asked to support their assertions, most advocates haul out letters of effusive praise from past participants. Beyond that, they insist that the whole thing is just so "logical" and makes so much "intuitive sense" that there can be no doubt as to whether the learning will "transfer" — that is, that it will be valuable back on the job.

Whither Training Transfer?

Granted, I accept the worth of an awful lot of management training on the basis of no more ironclad "proof" than that. But the Tarzan transfer? I'm inclined to say, "Sure, if your job is leading executive retreats in the woods or making Eagle Scout. Otherwise, mark me absent."

The advocate's response? That I scoff because I *fear* the mountain, the river, the forest primeval. I fail to understand that learning to overcome such existential terror is the very warp and woof of the managers-in-the-woods experience.

Well, actually, some of those tree-top rope swings and slide-for-life rigs look like a hoot to me. I have loved jumping out of airplanes and white-water rafting and rappelling down cliffs. Give me more! But as much fun as such things are in and of themselves, I can't honestly point to a single hair-raising episode that has, by analogy, taught me something so important about life or work that I would presume to drag you through it so you could share in the enlightenment.

Another thing: Why is the range of metaphorical learning options always so narrow — and, let's face it, so hedonistic? Why do so many other worth-while opportunities get missed in favor of cavorting in the North Woods? When the Mississippi River was flooding communities up and down its length, I didn't hear a single report of a training program called "dike constructions for team development." How about a weekend in post-hurricane Florida doing "roof repair and garage raising for advanced communication and planning training?"

But then again, you wouldn't be guaranteed a hot shower and a low-cal gourmet meal at the end of the day — only the chance to get out of yourself and do something as good for your soul as it is for your skills.

It's been said — wisely, I think — that the most productive management training brings together real management teams and has them work on real business problems in real time. No, it's not the only productive way to train managers, but the further you get from that ideal, the more you ought to question what you're really accomplishing. ■

Woo-Woo on Runway One-Niner

I t's like a returning plague of locusts. Every decade or so, we are treated to a high-profile visitation of woo-woo training. In the 1960s — yes, there was training in the '60s — we had the great T-group flap, also known as the sensitivity-training fiasco. The dawning of the Age of Aquarius brought with it pressure for managers to be more people-oriented and less concerned with production. A couple of *Life* magazine stories lauded the trend, and before you could say "blind trust walk," the corporate world was knee-deep in sensitivity trainers. Most were qualified to be sensitivity trainers by virtue of having attended a weekend retreat themselves, and having read at least one article on the subject.

Before long managers were being trucked off to woodsy lodges and suburban conference centers, and there encouraged to reveal their deepest secrets and insecurities to their colleagues — all in the name of becoming more sensitive to others and more tuned in to themselves. People naive enough to take the group leaders at their word bared their souls. Then they returned to the same old work environments — emotionally "outed." Stories of sudden resignations were fairly common. Eventually the press turned a jaundiced eye on the movement, and the fervor subsided.

> *Managers were trucked off to woodsy lodges and encouraged to reveal their deepest secrets.*

The 1980s saw a resurgence of woo-woo under the banner of reinventing organizational visions and values. Concerns arose over the philosophical and religious values allegedly embedded in some corporate training programs. Opponents objected that these courses trafficked in spiritual issues that were well outside the realm of legitimate job-related training.

The most high-profile complaint was aimed at a program developed by consultant Charles Krone for Pacific Bell, the San Francisco-based phone company. The jargon-heavy "Kroning" process, as the program became known in the company and the press, was based in part on the thinking of a mystic philosopher named Georges Gurdjieff. Complaints resulted in a 1987 investigation by the California Public Utilities Commission and a great deal of embarrassment for the company.

Past is prologue, and the woo-woo bunny has again hopped onto the scene. The most recent case involves the Federal Aviation Administration and some peculiar activities conducted in the name of cultural diversity training.

According to an internal FAA investigation begun in 1993, the flap concerns training programs conducted by two consulting firms, Gregory May and Associates of Sacramento, CA, and the Hart Performance Group Inc. of

Baltimore. A male air-traffic controller in Aurora, IL, filed a sexual harassment suit against the FAA last September as a result of the Hart training. He alleges he was forced to walk a gauntlet of women who patted his crotch and taunted him with sexually suggestive comments. Several hundred FAA employees reportedly were subjected to the same educational experience.

Details of the May and Associates program are more vague. Phrases like "guru mind control" surfaced recently on Ted Koppel's "Nightline." Other news reports suggest that program participants were tied together, screamed at, and deprived of sleep. According to Secretary of Transportation Federico Peña, executives responsible for these questionable training programs are being disciplined or reassigned.

It appears that the rise and fall and rebirth of woo-woo is inevitable in the training business. What with the high turnover among both gurus and gullible managers, it's difficult to see how to break the cycle. But here for your consideration are five rules of thumb that at least may keep your name out of the tabloids:

Five Ways to Stay Out of the Headlines

1. Any program that requires trainees to endure an experience that even remotely resembles Marine Corps basic training, a gulag work camp, or a fraternity Hell Week should be viewed with extreme skepticism.

2. Likewise any program that depends entirely on the teachings of a single guru — be it B.F. Skinner, W.E. Deming or Edgar Cayce. This is particularly true if the enthusiasts (sellers) contend that only those disciples who personally have touched the robes of the holy one can presume to conduct the "teaching."

3. When the question, "What will they be able to do at the end of the program that they can't do now?" is met with answers like, "One cannot explain the purpose of the teachings, one must experience them to understand," it is advisable to reach for the long cuffed leather gloves and a forked stick. Boots are assumed.

4. Any program that asks trainees to reveal their views on sensitive sociopolitical issues or to describe their basic spiritual or religious beliefs should be looked at askance — even if the promoters tell you all such revelatory acts are strictly voluntary. When people are sent to a program by their employer, there is no such thing as "voluntary." The interpersonal pressure to participate is enormous.

5. If the use of an arcane vocabulary defines who is in the know and who isn't, re-examine the core concepts of the program. Chances are, you're being offered old wine in funny-colored new bottles. If so, just dust off your last version of the program instead of paying for this one.

Trying to save managers from bouts of temporary insanity is a thankless and generally unrewarding task. If you can simply give them a chance to take a deep breath and notice that their marbles are rolling around on the floor, maybe that's all you can hope for. ■

The Training Stage: On a Goofy Day, Wand-Waving Outweighs Competence

The Monday morning mail should have been warning enough: On top of the in-box was a six-inch pile of "Letters to the Editor." Letters one through three were of a common sort. The old "not only did you guys hit the nail on the head, but I'll bet your readers would love to know that my company offers a (program, survey, process, etc., ad nauseum, ad infinitum) that is designed to cure every problem you so astutely pointed out in your article!"

Letters four and five "viewed with alarm that you purported to write a comprehensive article on this critically important area without mentioning the ground-breaking, industry-leading work of (my client, my boss, our founder, *moi*). You've shortchanged readers and denigrated the industry."

Go buy an ad boys and girls; that's what I do.

Numero six praised an article's insight; seven said this about the same article: "The biggest load of crap I've ever read. Cancel my subscription." Number eight had a bit of personal sting attached. It was about something I had recently co-scribbled and was proud of, an article called "Customers From Hell." The letter said it was unjust, unhealthy, unfunny, and un-Christian. Didn't I understand, it asked, that to a true believer, "Hell is too serious a concept to make light of." Baloney! It was funny; my mother said so!

> *Ya gotta hope it's a fluke when a competent trainer loses out on a job for lack of "perkiness."*

Can You Believe It?

But the primo goofiness of the day came in a you-won't-believe-this-commiseration with a friend who just had been turned down for a management training job. The friend had been with a large company for several years, lost his training director spot — as a Christmas present — in a cost-cutting frenzy, and has been on the hunt for months. Anyway, Charlie had stopped holding out for a comparable slot last month, shortly after the severance ran out. He rewrote his résumé, and has been interviewing for stand-up trainer slots.

Seems Charlie was one of the three finalists auditioning for the part. Auditioning? Well, what else would you call a job interview that required applicants to teach their favorite supervisory unit? And for free! But that isn't the unbelievable part. In fact, I though the audition bit made some sense, given how hard it is to assess stand-up training skills in an interview.

The "Ye Gods!" part was that Charlie, a guy with one master's degree in school psychology and another in industrial relations, lost the job because, as judge number four explained, *"You just aren't perky enough."* Really. That's

what she said. "Because you aren't perky enough." Wait! Wait! There's more! When Charlie showed up for the audition, he was led to a classroom, given a "wand" (one of those clear plastic tubes filled with sparkle and glycerin) and a box of foam squares to throw at students "to encourage participation" as he was told. This is the literal truth, so help me God. He also was given crayons and newsprint for the trainees to use to "express themselves emotionally." Can't you see it: right in the middle of a heated discussion about the legal aspects of employee performance review a frustrated trainee whips out his newsprint and Crayola pack and draws a stick figure version of "Horatio at the Bridge" in fuchsia and yellow. Hello Freud!

I don't know about you, but I don't think I would have done much better than Charlie; too much giggling from the instructor just ain't dignified. And I haven't the foggiest idea who would have been able to teach a credible class worrying about when and how to bewitch the trainees with a wand, or when to throw the old foam cubes around. Just too bloody much creative pressure.

Charlie isn't sure they actually use all that gear in the company's supervisory training. It may just have been a test to see if Charlie was flexible, creative, and quick on his feet. Of course, the examiners explained with great sincerity that the corporate CPAs and MBAs are intent upon loosening up the old corporate culture and putting some fun into the way things are done at old Spacely Sprockets.

I know I'm getting too old for this business. And I'm way too cynical. But I'm ruined for honest work. And besides, every time I start to get bored or begin to believe that I've seen everything under the sun, I have a day like this and realize that I ain't seen half of nothin' yet. Ye Gods, the fun has just begun. ■

Have You Seen Your Best Training Days? Check Yourself Against These 15 Indicators

S ome people don't know when to say when. Aging boxers, dancers, singers, and politicians come quickly to mind. No matter how many times the world sees and comments derisively on the spectacle of an Ali or Foreman climbing between the ropes long after his midriff is too ample to make the trip, there is always one more in line, looking for that one last shot at fleeting fame.

Operatic star Joan Southerland knew when her pipes were going and how to make a graceful exit. Too bad the Beach Boys don't share the same gift for self-assessment. Dr. "J" knew when to give up basketball, but Kareem, well, a year earlier would have been a lot classier. But coaches, teammates and agents sometimes keep you from making the wisest decisions.

But in truth, it's easier for dancers and boxers and ballplayers to know when the party is winding down. You can make the play or you can't. With CEOs, politicians, and training directors, it's harder to tell. Most CEOs are covered by mandatory retirement rules. Still, some hang on long after the executive dining room staff has started cutting their custard into bite-sized pieces.

The fifth time your new employee orientation program comes back for updating, it may be time to consider the exit door.

How will you know when you've been a training director long enough and it's time to move over, move on or move out? For myself, I've always used the *Principle of Unending Tasks* (PUT) as helpful criteria. PUT holds that most projects never really finish — they just stop for lack of interest or money. Take training program development. No matter how many pilot tests you run, programs always go "on line" with bugs in them. And even those that are done well enough to fool everybody come back to you for revisions as soon as somebody in engineering changes a screw spec or somebody in operations decides that selling isn't a part of a teller's job after all. That usually happens around 10 minutes after you start the roll out.

So my rule of thumb was that the fifth time the "Basic Selling Skills" or the "New Employee Orientation" programs landed back in my shop for major overhaul and modernization, it was time to consider going gently into that good, good night. Maybe that's just me. Others may look forward to doing the same project over again for the rest of their days, and way beyond their dotage.

I decided to find out how others in the T&D biz decide that it's time to travel on — or put the suitcases away all together. During a *TRAINING*

Magazine conference, I conducted an intensive focus group session at the Blue Note Conference Center and Cafe in downtown New York City. What follows are the considered thoughts of seven eminent current and former training directors on sure warning signs that it's time to consider moving on. Take them in the spirit and the light in which they were made:

---

15 Signs That Your Time Has Come

1. You mention your mentor to a new trainer and she asks if he's still living.
2. All the names in your Rolodex are crossed out.
3. When you go on the road, the first two things you pack are support hose and orthopedic shoes.
4. An employee you still think of as "the kid" makes an appointment to discuss early retirement — his.
5. While interviewing a candidate for a senior trainer slot, you learn you once interviewed the candidate's father.
6. Your idea of time management is remembering not to take Maalox and Metamucil in the same day.
7. You get winded making a To-Do list.
8. You know all the answers but can't remember the questions.
9. You look forward to paperwork.
10. You realize you are managing the 17th update of the new employee orientation program.
11. You need a rest break while dialing international phone calls.
12. You start burning the midnight oil at about 9 p.m.
13. You go to lunch with a vendor and the wait person tells you there is a 10 percent senior discount.
14. Your pacemaker keeps opening your garage door.
15. Your mind makes appointments your memory can't keep.
16. Your idea of exercise is spreading rubber cement on your desk and rolling fake boogers for an hour.
17. You can't reliably count to 15 anymore.

Funny Business: Training Still Has Its Share of Snake Oil — and Sincerity

After 25 years, you'd think I'd be bored with the average training industry trade show. Just the opposite. I really look forward to these scrambles — especially the exhibit halls.

Those halls are the one place, other than the drink-ticket socials, where I am likely to run into old cronies. Some as exhibitors, some as gawkers.

Then there's the improvisational entertainment. I dearly enjoy wandering the aisles and watching first-time trade show sales reps attempting to hook, net, and land the conventioneers as they school by. Little do they know how slippery and elusive their prey can be. Even when boated, the wily training pro can flip out of grasp and away to safe waters with nary a ripple of evidence.

And on the rare occasion when I allow myself to be reeled over the gunwales into a trade show booth, the fun really begins. No, I don't ask snot-nosed questions. I just listen and do a lot of "Uhuh-ing" and positive head shaking. It's a lot like listening to third-graders sing the "Start Spankled Banana" on parents' day. The tune is great, but the words tend to make no sense.

> *Whatever ails you, there's someone who's got the cure — real or otherwise.*

The last time I swam an exhibit hall I learned that, "The behavioralist (sic) ideas pretty much died with Bob Skinner," that "The Management Grid is pretty much a personality test," and that "according to research in *TRAINING Magazine*, half the *Fortune* 500 companies will do the majority of their training via computer-based courses." (For the record: 1. He ain't Bob; 2. It isn't a personality test; and 3. *TRAINING* never said that.)

Every trade show has at least one vendor promising programs that "never existed before," and have arrived "just in time to save your training souls."

Inevitably, I spend a couple of hours with these new brooms, earnestly fulfilling my reportorial duties. "You better write this down and put it in your magazine," they admonish. *"Our mission, Ron, is nothing less than to change the way training is done in corporate America."*

What fascinates me is the consistency in rap and image over 25 years of watching them come and go. I am reminded of a scene from *The Music Man*, wherein the noon train rolls into River City, and Professor Harold Hill goes into his famous opening pitch:

"Well, my friends, you got trouble, right here in Training City, with a capitol 'T' and that rhymes with 'P' and that stands for plain (trouble, trouble, trouble, trouble).

"Friends, have you noticed the telltale signs of training trouble creeping into your classrooms? Students snoring or staring into space...newspaper reading behavior exhibited during your best video show...spitball throwing during data feedback. Well that means trouble, trouble, trouble right here in Training City, with a capitol 'T' which rhymes with 'B' which stands for 'Bored.'

And the cure, Professor?

"Why, we've hired the best artists, the best writers, the best video producers, and the best instructional technologists to produce a quality product the likes of which this industry has never seen before!"

And I'm almost always convinced the professor — er, salesperson — is well-intentioned, hard-working, clever, sincere — and spending his spare time interviewing architects for the winter place he intends to build on Maui when he sells his gig for a nice premium to a larger interest.

In the end, 99 percent of these new kids burn through their start-up bankroll 10 times faster than they anticipated, book a lot fewer sales than lunches, and remember that they had actually meant to go into the garden tool catalog business instead.

At the same time, it's uncanny how mom-and-pop training entrepreneurs, with the industrial strength, staple-bound handouts and a pocketful of markers, seem to keep rolling along.

So what's the secret to success in the big-time training business? Darned if I know. I'm the guy who, a couple of years ago, unabashedly told a big-time video producer his 90-minute video, *In Search of Another Best Seller*, featuring Professor Shlemp of Big Deal Eastern University lecturing the CEOs of the world on their shortcomings, was destined to fail — the week before it hit $3 million in sales.

What I do know is that this is a fun and funny business, with enough twists and turns, egos and excesses, and some awfully bright and concerned professionals to keep a body interested for a heck of a long time. ■

Trainers, Prepare for Your New Role As...Gender Familiarity Monitor

Q uestion: Is an organization accountable for the unwelcome flirtatious behavior on the part of its employees?

A nswer: The courts, a variety of government agencies, and current common practice have pretty much answered that one in the affirmative. It's well-defined in the literature as sexual harassment, and the employer is responsible for taking steps to keep it from occurring and to punish it if it does happen. Period.

But what about zealously consensual, libidinous behavior? Is there a legitimate organizational interest in who is dining and dancing, flirting and romancing with whom — beyond the grist of coffee break gossip?

Earlier in this century schoolteachers, ministers, accountants, and people in "responsible positions" could lose their jobs for such untoward conduct as smoking cigarettes and drinking alcohol (in public or private), cursing, spitting, or dressing unbecomingly — not to mention courting without proper supervision. Times change and the current conventional wisdom has, by and large, held that what consenting adults consent to do or with one another — off the job and away from the office anyway — is more or less none of the organization's beeswax.

Employers are responsible for taking steps to keep sexual harassment from occurring — and to punish it if it does.

That wonderfully clean and simple formula may, however, be headed for the scrap heap based on the outcome of a lawsuit recently filed against Royal Bank of Canada. The plaintiff in this case alleges that the bank is a culpable correspondent to the demise of his previously blissful marriage. The plaintiff charges that the bank, his now ex-wife's employer, required the same said lady to work late hours and weekends and in general facilitated her coming to "know" a male coworker so well that the aforementioned "knowledge" became somewhat Biblical in nature, and that this tryst led to the acrimonious end of a happy marriage.

Oh, the Ramifications

Should the plaintiff win his case, the potential ramifications are mind boggling. From the corner Dairy Queen to the labs of Microsoft, a policy morass will ensue as supervisors and trainers everywhere will be thrust unwillingly into the new role of...Gender Familiarity Monitor.

Sample this scenario:

Ron, the supervisor: "James and Sally, I've asked you to meet with me to discuss a developing situation that is potentially a violation of our new anti-intimacy policy."

James and Sally: "How's that Ron?"

Ron: "Well, you two have been working closely on several projects over the last 30 days and we have no 402.6T on file for either of you."

J&S: "A 402.6T, Ron?"

Ron: "That's right. Also referred to as the UMSTCA. Short for the Unsupervised Mixed Sex Travel Consensus Acknowledgment form. Your spouses must acknowledge that you are traveling and working in close proximity with a member of the opposite sex and that they have no objections. Oh, and I also see here that neither of you has signed the ROLF-UCA-FUCC."

J&S: "The what?"

Ron: "A Release of Liability for Unfortunate Consequences Arising from Unauthorized Consensual Contact."

Special Problems for Trainers

Worse yet will be the problems some trainers encounter in this new landscape, particularly those with a propensity for participative sessions and off-site venues:

Prosecutor: "And so Mr. Trainer, will you explain to the jury the purpose of these exercises you forced Jim and Sally to participate in while at the Bidawee Lodge? Did you not demand that Jim and Sally and others of the Acme Widgets executive team take part in something called 'Trust Falls' where they were encouraged to leap into each others' arms?"

Trainer: "Well, sort of but…"

Prosecutor: "And did you not encourage them to take long walks in the woods?"

Trainer: "Well, yes…"

Prosecutor: "And was not one member of each of these strolling couples blindfolded and therefore required to hold hands and come to depend on and lean on their partner for support?"

Trainer: "Yes, but you see…"

Prosecutor: "And in view of all this forced intimate contact between these men and women, do you still contend that you, as an agent for Acme Widgets, are not directly responsible for the romantic dalliance that came about as a result?"

Those of you who specialize in "harder" skills, like say circuit-board training, may be laughing up your sleeve at these potential problems. But hold on there just one second. Aren't your little lecturettes on 'flux selection' just, you know, a little bit racy? And aren't those soldering tools and all that welding equipment, aren't they, you know, just a little bit, well, superfluously Freudian? And are you absolutely sure that… ■

Few Are Safe in This New Copyright-Crazed World

The information-as-commodity age is upon us. As a result, we find ourselves in an entrepreneurial, up-for-grabs, nothing-should-surprise-us economy. Every walking, talking, get-rich-in-a-hurry-without-breaking-a-sweat wanna-be is out there with a ball of twine and a couple of sticks staking out "intellectually protectable" territory with the fervor of a pack of California gold seekers at Sutter's Mill in 1849.

To wit: A sculptor here in Minneapolis is suing Warner Bros. for an unspecified load of money because a sculpture of his appears briefly in the background of a shot in the *Batman Forever* movie. His argument, as best as I can understand it, is that while he sold the sculpture to the person who put it into the movie's background, *he did not sell his copyright to the work.* Ergo, he believes Warner Bros. owes him a truckload every time the movie is shown someplace in the known universe.

When they start copyrighting motorcycle sounds, you know things are out of hand.

Last year, *USA Today* reported that doctors are patenting their "processes" and "procedures" and demanding other doctors who use them obtain a license and pay a royalty. Case in point is an Arizona opthamologist named Samuel Pallin who developed a unique incision for cataract surgery, which he patented with the U.S. Office of Patents — and subsequently sued a competing physicians' group that incorporated his cutting-edge "cut" in its surgical bag of tricks.

And a recent issue of *The Wall Street Journal* informs that Harley-Davidson Co. has filed an application with the U.S. Patent and Trademark Office for exclusive rights to — get this — its motorcycle engine sound. The sound is said to roughly resemble someone with a basso voice urgently repeating the word potato, as in *potato-potato-potato-potato.* The company already holds a copyright for the word "Hog."

Stop Me Before I Copyright Again

I myself have frequently run afoul of this idea that anything and everything you think up should be protected and reserved for you as the "thinker-upper" — and that anyone who thinks the same thought owes you money for the privilege thereof.

I have in former years convinced myself (and others) that it didn't make sense that some people could, just because they decided to, mark off as private property a piece of a language that has been around since the Stone Age. But it is becoming apparent that this is a battle I am destined to lose.

So like my Great Grandaddy Henry Franklin Rose, who at the conclusion of the War Between the States qualified for a pension from both the North and South, I have decided to stop swimming against the tide and switch sides.

My partners and I now have in the works the reservation and trademarking of the following terms, phrases, and processes for use in the training market by and for ourselves alone:

(1) "Tell Me More About That™"

This is a unique, carefully constructed interrogative for inducing interactive participation from sapient life forms in a classroom setting. And while it has admittedly been in common use for some years, we nonetheless believe that our unique enunciations and research-based "gesture set" make this dynamic technology uniquely identifiable with our organization alone. (Licensing terms available upon request.)

(2) "Roll Play™"

A technique for creating interpersonal closeness between people who have no more in common than a group of wayward Albanian tourists on a bus trip across the former Yugoslavia in search of a fire-free zone.

It consists in part, but not entirely, of bringing together seven to 1,700 individuals and one rectangular table upon which has been placed one superheated carafe of decaffinated coffee, one carafe of room temperature caffinated coffee, 100 individual serving-sized containers of DairlyLike™ flavoring product, and one tray of 1" x 1" squares of two-day-old sugared Breadlike™ product.

Several pieces of our already copyrighted *Getting to Know You Technology*™ are enfolded into the dynamics of Roll Play™ interaction management, including but not limited to our patent-pending "Hi! My Name Is ____" software.

(3) "TentCard™"

This is an 8 x 10-inch sheet of 75-pound weight, buff-colored, 88 percent reflective pressed pulp material, center-folded on the long dimension to create an isosceles triangle or "tent"-shaped structure which, in proper context, is utilized to identify by name participants in an educationally oriented event.

If you have any information as to the copyright, trademark, or patent status of any of these, I would be pleased to hear from you, as our legal fees currently are 7 percent higher than our year-to-date earnings and we are exploring options for Reengineering™ our current system for trademarking our processes and techniques. ■

Then Again, Maybe You'd Rather Be Selling Knives at the State Fair

There's an outfit in New York called Research Alert that did a survey and came to the conclusion that you don't like your job very much. Well, what the survey really found was 51 percent of all working people said they would choose a different line of work if they could start over again. So that means that one of us — either you or me — doesn't like our job. And since I don't have a job — at least that's what the guy next to me on a plane recently said when I explained to him what I do for a living — it must be you who wants to start over again.

In any case, we all know we can't really go back and start over, but having thought long about this problem, I conclude the next best thing would be to evaluate current skills, strengths, and weaknesses and then determine what fields offer a reasonable chance of success for folks with our skills and experience.

There are really only five safe and sane alternatives to the training jobs we now hold.

Some career development counselors will try to convince us that all we have to do is think for a minute to realize we probably already possess the skills we need for any job. I think these people get paid by the number of informational lunches their "counselees" talk other people into. They are no doubt paid by the National Restaurant Association.

There are also hundreds of motivational speakers out there preaching some variation of, "If you can see it, you can be it. You can accomplish anything in the known universe if you will only set your mind to it." I disagree. It says "S" on my jockey shorts and I know for a fact that regardless of how much they need the help, the Los Angeles Lakers are not going to make me their first-round draft choice no matter how badly I want them to.

So in the name of efficiency, I am eliminating all such absurd career longings. I've come down to five safe, sane, appropriate, and appealing replacements for training jobs now held and hated.

1. President and chief executive officer of a savings and loan.

The Resolution Trust Corp. has a number of opportunities available just waiting for the right people to snap them up. No qualifications whatsoever are required, except a promise to try harder than the last owner. I make this suggestion because it's widely known that RTC is considering taking IRA and 401K plans in trade for available institutions. In Houston, they took a '57 Chevy and a collection of 1972 Lichtenstein first-day covers for a three S&L combo.

2. Day-care center management.

While some people argue this career recommendation should be restricted only to those experienced in educating executives, I disagree. I think anyone who has managed a staff of classroom training specialists, an audiovisual department, or produced a videotape of a sweaty-upper-lipped CEO giving a "Spirit of Partnership" message to the troops is equally qualified. Uniquely qualified also is anyone who has held a full-time job of any sort for five years or more while raising two kids to their age of majority with no major arrests or convictions.

3. Internationally known consultant and soon-to-be-published best-selling book author.

This a qualified recommendation. This career is only distinguishable from unemployment by the cost of a box of business cards and what is written on the forms at visits to the local office of the state department of employment and training.

4. Maitre d' at a restaurant with an unpronounceable made-up French-sounding name.

Again, a qualification. The best of these jobs are found in big-deal cities such as New York, Washington, San Francisco, Los Angeles, Miami, Toronto, and Montreal. There are few, by comparison, in Indianapolis, Kansas City, Little Rock, Ottawa, or Vancouver. That owing, no doubt, to the fact that not many people in these "less-culturally knowledgeable" cities are genuinely excited to spend exaggerated sums of money for the privilege of being insulted by bored art-school dropouts and eating wilted red cabbage leaves drizzled with olive oil.

The basic qualifications, however, are definitely in our skill bags. Most important is the ability to purge from memory all the customer service techniques and skills we've taught others — and the desire to get even with everyone who has ever insulted or brow beaten us in former lives.

5. Ginzu knife demonstrator on the State Fair circuit.

Afraid of knives? OK, you can substitute genuine hand-hammered, just-in-from-the-heart-of-China wok cookers. Think of the natural fit: Communicating with people from a rich variety of backgrounds, the thrill of direct sales, and the opportunity to enlighten and enrich the lives of thousands.

I hope this list of new career opportunities for trainers exiting the profession is as exciting and promising to you as it is to me. And, of course, if we network this just right, we should be able to unearth dozens more opportunities to enrich our lives through new and exciting vocations. ■

Recipe for Overkill:
One Part Simple Idea,
Two Parts Marketing Hype

I felt guilty filling out the entry form for the Publishers' Clearing House Sweepstakes. After all, I was going to be getting this $10 million check handed to me on the morning of Aug. 11, 1995, by this Mr. David Sayer, executive director of the Publishers' Clearing House Prize Patrol, and I had never bought even a single magazine, book, videotape, or crossword puzzle from the man's organization. I mean, it could get pretty uncomfortable standing there on my front stoop in my Donald and Mickey Get Ready For School bathrobe, with that camera in my unshaven face, trying to say something without revealing my disloyalty:

"Oh my god! I can't possibly accept this $10 million because all those years you have been patiently sending me those entry forms I have never accepted my responsibility in this relationship and so much as ordered a single, cancel-at-any-time, free-trial issue of even one of your bargain-priced magazines."

Even the best ideas can become miscreants when taken to extremes by people overeager to extend a product line.

To preclude such an embarrassing scenario I decided to at least peruse the sheet of perforated stamps that constitute the list of Publishers' Clearing House offerings.

There were good deals on *PC Magazine* and *Computer World*, but I passed. I have enough trouble with computers in the office and don't need to be hounded about my inadequacies at home. The same for *Trolls: The Magazine of Effective Client Relations*.

I would have liked to have added *Popular Photography* or *Golf Digest* or *Field & Stream* or even *Flower & Garden* to the hobbyist, humor, and news magazines we already receive, but it has rained here in Minnesota for 117 consecutive weekends and, well, who wants to pay to be reminded that on other parts of the continent people are actually experiencing something resembling summer.

More Joys of Jell-O

I was about to give up and say that I had done my duty as an entrant when I spied a stamp for a cookbook called *More Joys of Jell-O*. This excited and stunned me because obviously if there is a book called *More Joys of Jell-O* there first had to be a book called *Joys of Jell-O* that had sold enough copies for the publisher to commission a sequel — the *Terminator 2 of Jell-O* preparation guides.

I rushed to my kitchen to find a package of Jell-O to see if I had been underrating its complexities and subtleties. All I could find were three packets of Knox brand unflavored gelatin. On the back of each envelope was a different recipe calling for the use of "1 envelope Knox Unflavored Gelatin." The "Classic Almond Cream" and the "Luscious Cappuccino Frosting" seemed simple enough. Both began: "In small saucepan, sprinkle unflavored gelatin over water; let stand one minute. Stir over low heat until completely dissolved." But the "Classic Tomato Aspic" recipe was a different story:

"In a large bowl," it began unassumingly enough, "sprinkle unflavored gelatin (three packets this time) over cold tomato juice; let stand one minute." Then came the twist, the unpredictable turn of the spoon that made it clear we're dealing here with an art form of infinite and subtle variety: "Add hot juice and stir until gelatin is dissolved, about five minutes." Well, you can just tell where this is going! Sometimes water, sometimes juice. Sometimes hot, sometimes cold. Sometimes one minute, sometimes five. All that variety. No wonder the poor publisher had no choice but to yield to reader pressure and commission a *Son of Joys of Jell-O*.

More Flip Charts and You

If that sort of variety is possible for something as seemingly simple as the use of gelatin foods, think of the possibilities for you and me in the vastly more complicated field of human resource development. How about *Flip Charts and You*, followed by *More Flip Charts and You*, and reprised yet again in *Advanced Flip Chart Techniques and You*. And that's just the print media. I can easily envision the "I Flip Over Flip Charts" T-shirt.

I could go on and on, but you'll have to wait for publication of my home study course, "How to Create a Livelihood Out of a Single Simple Idea" and its sequel, "How to Find or Borrow a Single Simple Idea to Make a Livelihood Out Of." There will be three workbooks, four audiotaped lectures, and a 900 number to call for continuing consultation...The potential is simply boundless. ■

How to Succeed in Consulting Without Really Trying

Maybe your company has just downsized you out of a job, handing you a nice separation package to cushion the blow of your seat bouncing on the pavement. Or maybe you've just been reflecting on that time last fall when you gave the speech on "The Total Quality Approach to Widget Winding" at the National Association of Widget Manufacturers' Annual Conference in Las Vegas, and that high-ranking exec from the biggest player in your industry shook your hand and told you that you were doing inspiring, world-class work. Whatever the reason, you are seriously considering hanging out a shingle, forming a Subchapter S corporation, and turning yourself into a full-fledged consultant in the training-and-development field. Just one question:

Are you crazy?

It's cold out here! It's dog-eat-dog. For the first two or three years you'll never know where your next mortgage payment is coming from. We're talking long nights. Exploitive clients who will try to beat down your fee after the work is done and the product delivered. Competitors who won't think twice about ripping off your materials and peddling them to their own clients as if the stuff had just come down the mountain from Moses in a Fed-Ex overnight package.

It is a scientific fact that 82.7 percent of all people who go into independent consulting burn through the 18-month grubstake they've set aside in exactly 12 weeks, and end up selling self-improvement audiotapes door to door. That's during the day. Nights, you find them doing inventory at 7-Eleven stores.

What works for Madonna will work for you: Dumb it down.

Of the 17.3 percent who do make a go of consulting, half spend the first five years doing hand-me-down subcontracts for other consultants for about $7 an hour, and partying down on macaroni-and-cheese per diems.

Of course, you're sitting there saying to yourself, "Oh, I know all that, but it won't happen to me." Besides, you figure, why should you listen to this crap from some guy who, for 25 years, has been doing the very thing he's warning you away from? (One reason is that it took him most of those years just to reach an income bracket that consistently supports an IRA account. But never mind, you don't want to hear about it.)

Since you won't change your mind no matter what I say, here are a few hard-won lessons that might shorten your learning curve a bit and hasten your arrival in the wonderful world of big-time, high-paying consulting gigs.

Let's start with a few basic facts.

Hard-Won Lessons on Consulting

• It is important that you be a more or less skilled individual — that you are, in fact, able to do something in the human resources development (HRD) arena that somebody might conceivably pay you to do. And let's be clear here about what we mean by "a skill." We do not mean a facility for browning up to the right people, or for hiring bright people to work for you, though these talents are valuable and will serve you well in your new career.

That said, however, it is nonetheless important to have what we might call an "official" skill, one that provides the person whose backside you are kissing with a plausible excuse to hire you: instructing, writing scripts, administering surveys, analyzing performance problems, delivering punchy speeches, writing clearly on a chart pad, producing long reports...whatever. Furthermore, you will have to be able to prove to potential clients that at some time in your past, somebody has actually paid you to perform this skill — and not regretted the decision.

• You say you've been out teaching the 14 Deming Commandments and the Seven Magic Tools of Synergistic Teamwork, and everyone in your corporation or canasta club agrees that you are just about the smartest, the cutest, and the most supportive darned instructor they have ever had the privilege of watching waltz around a classroom? Wonderful! Just understand that none of that puts one dime in your pocket once you hang out your shingle and announce that you are now accepting clients.

• Regardless of how skillful you are, and no matter how many clients you think you have prequalified before you set up shop, the reality is that you will spend most of your time doing sales and marketing. All those people who thought you were so great when you worked for someone else? Now you've got to convince them that they ought to pay you to give them the advice you used to dish out for free over drinks after the association chapter meetings.

But Here's the Real Secret...

Most of the above is common sense. However, the following tips are — as they say on the late-night infomercials starring Charles "I Have More Cars Than You Do" Givens and Tony "I Have More Teeth Than You Do" Robbins — the simple but little-known secrets to consulting success that you will not find anywhere else in the known universe.

"How much will it cost me," you ask, "to gain access to these closely guarded success secrets heretofore known only to a select group of fabulously wealthy HRD consultants and the ancient Egyptian priests of Ra?" Well, dear reader, these precious pearls of wisdom are presented here not for the thousands of dollars you might expect to pay for the tapes and workbooks that are the usual repositories of such paradigm-altering information, not for the discounted hundreds of dollars you're sitting there hoping for, but absolutely free — free to you, our valued subscriber, from a publication grateful for your patronage.

Here, then, are the four cardinal secrets of consulting success.

Success Secret #1:
Not All Consulting Is Created Equal

There are three entirely different types of consulting. You must consider these types carefully in order to position yourself in the noisy, crowded, but essentially smoke-free marketplace of the independent consultant.

A **Type I or *Grunt* consultancy** entails doing actual work; that is, directly exercising your skills — the official ones — on behalf of your clients. This means teaching, interviewing and surveying customers or employees, writing manuals or job aids and so on. Essentially, it means doing day labor in the same field you used to harvest, but for far less money. (True, your hourly rate will rise, but try adding back the cost of the benefits you just gave up for the "freedom" of being your own person and deciding what work you will or won't deign to do — which turns out to be any work you can get your hands on.)

As a Type I consultant, you will spend four to six hours a day looking for work to keep you busy next week, and six to 10 hours a day doing the work you found last week. You'll generally get Sunday mornings off and a vacation once every three years.

You almost certainly will have to begin your consulting career as a Grunt. The only excuse for remaining one, however, is that you have joined a large consulting firm rather than becoming an independent practitioner. This, of course, is really no different from having an actual job, except that the hours and benefits are worse, and all the interesting money goes to the founders and the sales force. You do, however, acquire a legitimate right to call yourself a consultant on your business card and at cocktail parties.

A **Type II or *True* consultant** must be skilled at the art of telling, rather than doing. Like a racetrack tipster, the Type II consultant gives advice about how a thing should be done, but never places a bet on a horse. It helps to be able to point out that you have, in the past, actually done the kind of work on which you are consulting, though a number of consultants have demonstrated that it is possible to get by with merely having read a book about the subject.

If you have never done the work you are telling your client how to do but you have conducted an academic study of the topic, this will give you great credibility with MBA managers: people who have never done any work of any kind, save attending meetings and blaming underlings for any problems that arise back on the job in their absence.

Sadly, however, academic research will not impress bona fide line managers. Line managers will give you the time of day only if (a) you have physical scars, (b) you have been a consultant to two or more companies that compete successfully with the line manager's firm or, (c) you are an accountant who has studied the actual cost of doing the work the line manager oversees, and you can tell him without hesitation what positions can be eliminated and whom to fire. This gives him an easy out when he hands people their pink slips: "Jane, you know you mean the world to me, but the damned consultant says you have to go. Best of luck in your next job."

"Scapegoat" is a time-honored and well-paying role for consultants — pretty good work if you can get it. On the whole, though, it is best not to work with line managers at all. Whenever possible, choose as your client an MBA-trained marketing manager.

Type III or *Guru* consulting is the ultimate in the game. The Guru is acknowledged as an "expert" in a broad and absolute sense — a being assumed to occupy a high seat in a known pantheon of expertise. The Guru consultant is not hired or retained, but called upon to assist — though being "on retainer" has a certain panache for client and consultant alike.

Guru status most commonly is acquired in one of four ways: (1) outliving or outlasting a significant number of people in your subfield of expertise — the Gertrude Stein phenomenon; (2) publishing something widely read or, better yet, widely not read but universally quoted; (3) working for or near someone known widely by a single name or a set of initials, as in, "She once wrote a speech for JFK" or "He once drove Drucker to the airport after a speech in St. Louis" — the Alice B. Toklas phenomenon; (4) running a large organization for a few years, during which you employ a good public-relations staff. Note that in this last approach to guruhood, it is not necessary to have run the organization successfully. Far more important is to have appeared in its television commercials. You also must be able to speak forcefully and glowingly about "my philosophy of management" to banquet groups, convention attendees, and *Fortune* magazine reporters.

The Guru consultant never actually consults with anybody about anything for more than a few hours — a couple of days, tops. Many of the grandest Type III consultants are, in fact, shills for a cadre of Type I and Type II consultants who are either on salary or who pay kickback fees to the Guru. The Type III consultant, more than anything else, is a public speaker and snake charmer. The biggest challenges to the Type III are to keep the act relatively fresh and to remember the name of the organization that has hired him to hold forth for the day. This is more difficult than it sounds, as active Type IIIs often address 80 to 100 audiences a year: "If it's Tuesday this must be the Tractor Tire Rebuilder's Association Convention and, boy, am I glad to be here with this great-looking group! And I love your baseball caps."

Success Secret #2:
Dumb Wins, Smart Loses

Overintellectualization has been the downfall of many an endeavor. This is particularly true of HRD consulting endeavors. Even if you plan to work in the highly theoretical and esoteric world of "Personal Growth Facilitation," with a subspecialization in the Prema Sai Baba's interpretation of the Bhagavad Gita, you are well-advised to do so in words and concepts appropriate to the intellectual level of Sally and her cat, Puff.

This is especially important in today's socioeconomic milieu. The point is concisely articulated by professor Joseph Queenan in the management-development section of the March 1994 issue of *Playboy* magazine:

"All has changed in the age of Beavis and Butthead, Ren and Stimpy, Wayne and Garth, and the guy who called that time-out for Michigan with

11 seconds left in the 1993 NCAA basketball final. Today, joyously stupid people such as Roseanne Barr and Madonna are revered as national treasures while canny opportunists such as Rush Limbaugh make their fortunes pretending to be morons. Truly, there has never been a better time to be stupid."

What works for Madonna will work for you. Dumb it down.

Success Secret #3:
Looking Good Is Better Than Being Good

This principle is almost transparent to the casual observer, and can easily be confused with the old saw that one never encounters "a second chance to make a good first impression." But looking good, as opposed to looking flashy, is a subtle art. This is because the definition of looking good is as ephemeral as a Paris dress-designer's vision of proper skirt lengths.

• **The right car.** Where once no consultant with more than half a brain would think of approaching, say, General Motors while owning a Ford, the what-you-drive standard is no longer measured in such terms. The key to proper automobile ownership today is simply to own a car that will neither threaten the masculinity of your male clients (no Bentley; no old, battered Jeep) nor frighten your female prospects (nothing with "Love Bandit" stenciled on the doors). The Yugo instantly called to mind by these criteria would be a mistake, however, since your automobile also must suggest that you are successful and wise. The answer to this dilemma, as to most of life's problems: an immaculately restored 1957 Chevrolet convertible.

• **The right office.** A real professional has a real office. But the mandate that you must, therefore, have a flashy, midtown office is definitely dated. The consultant with a dedicated home office is seen today as perfectly respectable. This is a dramatic switch, since historically, of course, the home-officing consultant has been regarded as either a fly-by-night operator or simply someone between jobs. Thanks to computers, modems and fax machines, today's home-officing professional can pose as a thoroughly modern hipster of the information highway, a self-sufficient yet broadly connected paladin in no need of the pretensions of a 40th-floor office suite or a toadying support staff to justify inflated billings. Note, however, that the impression works best if you live in a place like Telluride or Key West or Carmel. If your home office is in Duluth or Cleveland, people will assume you're between jobs.

The best of all possible offices is the one on the client's premises. This indicates that you are a significant player in the organization's affairs and well worth every penny your client showers upon you. It also ensures instant cooperation, since everyone will recognize immediately that you are senior management's "hatchet person."

• **Personal appearance.** Consultant clothing styles are in transition just now. The "power" clothes of the late 1980s are seen as suspect. Just the same, an appropriately expensive suit on a man or a woman can communicate a sense of power and authority. White shirts and silk blouses are always in style, as are shoes, bags and belts with names such as Gucci, Blass, Ferregamo and Amalfi.

A growing trend is Contrarian Dress. This strategy requires that you spend some time parked near your prospective client's offices with a camera and a good telephoto lens, but many successful consultants swear it is worth the effort. Suppose that after photographing 100 people entering the world headquarters of VeriStaid Global Insurance Inc. you determine that the unofficial but obviously approved uniform consists of suits by either Armani or Picone, shirts by Nordstrom, ties by Ferregamo, and shoes by Johnston and Murphy. You then, to communicate your stature as a true, deep-thinking change agent, approach the VeriStaid decision-makers dressed in a tweed jacket from the Perlman catalog, olive twill slacks from Lands' End, a blue cotton chambray shirt from L.L. Bean, cartoon-character tie from Warner Bros. or Disney, and Rockport shoes.

Word is that the Contrarian approach has proven effective in Chicago, Denver, Dallas and Toronto, but seldom in New York and never in Boston or Atlanta. Oddly enough, it seems to work quite well in Paris and London.

• **Accessories.** The briefcase, yesterday's quintessential consultant accessory, should today be avoided. Briefcases are now associated primarily with copy-machine repair persons and junior-management trainees who use them to transport bologna sandwiches.

For a few years there, the single manila envelope was considered quite an impressive prop due to its suggestion of unfettered mental prowess. But the advent of notebook computers and personal portable telephones has ruined all that. Today's best bet in the carry-along category is a canvas bag with shoulder strap just large enough to securely hold your notebook computer, your phone, your Official Airline Guide, your personal organizer, and a Mont Blanc pen. This ensemble will reinforce the message that you are high-tech, in-touch, efficient and well-off.

Just remember: Never, ever stoop under the weight of this stuff. No matter how high-tech the gadgetry in your sack, if you look like you're lugging around a 50-pound bag of rocks, you'll be marked forever as a Type I (Grunt) consultant.

There is, obviously, much more to looking good. We haven't touched on business cards, stationery, report writing, dining, or even weekend office wardrobe. But at least we've started you thinking, and that's half the battle — as long as you don't think too hard (see Success Secret #2).

Success Secret #4:
Write a Mediocre Book with a Clever Title

Writing a book does not guarantee success in consulting, but it can give you an opportunity to raise your rates, and it does equip you with something better to send to prospective clients than the laughably ugly brochure you are bound to produce with your new desktop-publishing software.

Writing a book is, of course, an ambitious endeavor, and there are certain protocols to observe.

First rule: Do not, under any circumstances, set out to write an original book, or one containing more than a single idea. Forget about trying to interest a publisher in a project covering a topic not currently on at least one business best-seller list. Business-book publishers are much more comfortable publishing the fifth title on, say, total quality or sexual harassment or power breakfasts, than the first. Acquisitions editors look for manuscripts addressing topics that are already doing well for some other publisher. This is known as "filling out the list," a prime subject of cocktail-party conversation at the annual American Booksellers Association conference.

Consider: In the 18 months following the 1982 publication of *In Search of Excellence*, there appeared exactly 584,694 business books with the words "in search" or "excellence" in the title or subtitle.

Today, nothing has changed but the buzzwords. Walk into your local Barnes & Noble or B. Dalton outlet and count the number of business book titles that feature the words "customer," "quality," "reengineering" or "reinventing" in the title.

Don't worry about Chapters 3 through 12 of your book. They will never be read, and can be used over again in your sequels.

A good way to determine what your book will be about, therefore, is to research the best-seller lists that publishers study. After *The New York Times* list, one of the most respected is published by the Harry W. Schwartz Bookshops of Milwaukee. Since most business book publishers are in New York and have, in fact, never been west of the Hudson River, the Schwartz listings are regarded as critical intelligence from the wilds of the American frontier.

A third important source of intelligence — such as it is — is *Publishers Weekly* magazine. This periodical is dedicated to shop talk among publishers and editors. Here, they tell one another what the best sellers are, why they are best sellers, and how clever they (the publishers) are to have published them. The magazine also contains lots of pictures of people attending parties at the last booksellers' convention and the Frankfurt Book Fair.

Second rule: Mediocrity sells. Here is a helpful formula for writing your book:

• Read and digest two current best sellers, underlining the most memorable passages.

• Copy these underlined passages onto index cards.

• Shuffle the cards.

• Proceed to your word processor and begin entering the core of your manuscript.

One effective alternative formula is the "Oldies but Goodies" approach. Here, you do not dwell on today's best sellers but on the chart-toppers of yesteryear. Reviews in back issues of *Business Week*, the Sunday *New York Times* and *TRAINING Magazine* will provide your best leads.

Go back 10 or 12 years. Books that were hot between, say, 1982 and 1985 are good bets for topics that can be refurbished and resold to a new generation of readers and publishers. It is, in fact, much easier to sell an old idea to a business-book acquisitions editor than you might suspect. For one thing, acquisitions editors with more than eight months of tenure are referred to in publishing houses as "senior staff." For another thing, there are no new topics in business-book publishing anyway; there is only hot and cold.

An example of the "Oldies but Goodies" strategy at work: In the early '80s, a clever journalist named Peter McWilliams, who had co-written a couple of books on meditation and stress relief, bought a personal computer. Recognizing an opportunity when he saw one, McWilliams wrote a best-selling guide called *The Word Processing Book*. The entire publishing world jumped on the bandwagon, and by 1985 Books in Print listed more than 1,700 titles concerned with personal computers. This appears to have been the market-saturation point; by 1986, you couldn't give away a manuscript on personal computers.

Saturation, however, is a temporary phenomenon. Want to guess the titles of the hottest-selling how-to books of 1991, 1992 and 1993? Start with *DOS for Dummies*. Add *WordPerfect for Dummies*, *PCs for Dummies*, *Word for Dummies*, *Windows for Dummies* and the *Illustrated Computer Dictionary for Dummies*. Toss in six more books with "For Dummies" in the title, and you will see why Dan Gookin, a would-be novelist who took up writing about computers in 1984 to put bread on the table, is today a multimillionaire writer/consultant/speaker who secretly owns the state of Idaho.

What with copyright laws and all, refurbishing somebody else's 10-year-old book can present a sticky situation. Be guided in this area by two key ethical principles: (1) Dumb down the technical parts; (2) Change all the Ronald Reagan references to Bill Clinton references.

The only real intellectual challenge you will face will be writing Chapters 1 and 2. In Chapter 1 you must state in dire terms the problem you are going to solve. This will require that you spend several hours reading the headlines and lead paragraphs of stories in *The Wall Street Journal*, *Forbes* and *USA Today*. It is also useful to suggest in your opening chapter that Peter Drucker, Warren Bennis, or an obscure economist from England forewarned us of this terrible problem in his last book.

Chapter 2 is where you sketch out the gist of your solution to the problem stated in Chapter 1. Here it is important to use very high-blown and energetic-sounding words — the sorts of words that can be picked up by book reviewers and business-magazine writers, allowing these worthies to sound smart without having to know what the words actually mean.

For instance, never say, "You need to figure out how to keep your doughnut company from going broke." Instead, say, "It is strategically imperative to participatively create and communicate your vision of the organization's leadership role in the elective breakfast- and break-food market segment."

You don't need to worry much about Chapters 3 through 12. They will never be read and can be used over again in your sequels.

Finally, your book needs a clever title. The title, in fact, is far more important than the content. So when creating a provocative title, don't be overly concerned with what your book is actually about. Never mind that your manuscript amounts to one more tedious rehash of the shortcomings of performance-appraisal forms. Think "Sharks." Think "Paradigms." Think "Orangutans."

An acceptable alternative is to create an imposing-sounding title by mixing and matching pieces of current business jargon. You may even be expected to come up with a preliminary list of titles for your publisher to market test. (This, in most publishers' eyes, is far more important than making sure the spelling is right or that the pages are numbered correctly.) To save you some time, we have compiled the handy "Book Title Generator" below. To use the Book Title Generator, pick one word at random from each of the three columns and join them together into a title.

Ideally, your book will become a best seller. But even if it sells only 10 copies (nine to you, one to your mom), it is well worth the effort because in the consulting world, "best seller" is a highly relative term. Originally the phrase was associated with a ranking on some recognized list of titles that consumers actually were buying in significant numbers. Today, "best seller" is used assertively by consultants and their publicists as a straightforward synonym for "book" — and sometimes even for "unpublished manuscript" or "I had three chapters all written and typed and everything, but the dog ate them."

So remember: Write the book, cultivate the look, play it dumb, be a Guru instead of a Grunt. There you have the fourfold path to bliss in the consulting business.

Too hard? Too complicated? Then here's my advice: Start with the '57 Chevy. Everything else will work itself out. ■

BUSINESS BOOK TITLE GENERATOR

A	B	C
1. Global	1. Quality	1. Systems
2. Total	2. Service	2. Management
3. Reinventing	3. Diversity	3. Teams
4. Modularized	4. Synergistic	4. Deployment
5. Virtual	5. Time-based	5. Excellence
6. Customer	6. Empowered	6. Partnerships

To use the book title generator, pick one word at random from each of the three columns and join them together into a title.

The Mostly True Adventures of Cousin Jolly and Them Friends of His

There are those who do not believe in my Cousin Mavis's boy Jolly. Or if they do believe, they don't approve of his methods and ambitions. And though Jolly's various adventures as a personal development entrepreneur have made him well-off financially, there are still others who do not see him in any way as respectable.

He knows this. It does not trouble him, however, as he believes the doubters and the troubled among you are but a one-weekend retreat away from getting your lives truly turned around and your attitudes readjusted to the positive. For which you will only be charged a small fee, like everybody else, and with which comes two meals plus snack, accommodations, as well as a copy of his latest book, *Success Made Simple*, which you will certainly treasure all the more once you have received the insights of that life-affirming experiential adventure at his camp out on Inspiration Creek Reservoir. (There are those who have questioned the sincerity of Jolly's mission because of this money thing. But as Jolly's mentor and spiritual guide the Maharaja Mashies Gene has taught us, "Them that don't pay, don't get turned around. It ain't right or wrong. It's just the rule.")

But I am getting way ahead of myself here. Jolly has made a special plea to me to put down on paper his continuing story as I have come to know and understand it: from my point of perspective as a so-called professional journalist and as his second cousin twice removed on his Momma's side. So as to make this all make sense, we should start off somewhere near the beginning.

William Jefferson Clinton and the Birth of Talkin' Southern Seminars Inc.

Though I grew up in the state of Illinois, near the great wide-shoulder city of East Chicago, much of my roots and kin are in the more southern region of the state, near Anna. And then, too, we have kin strung out from there on down through Missouri, Tennessee, Kentucky, and Arkansas. I tell you this only to point out that though I am by geography and job a Northerner, much of my kin and genealogy are as Southern as chitlins and coon dogs.

I have known of and visited with Cousin Mavis a goodly many times as we are contemporary, and in the summers my immediate family would make a point of driving down to the big Rose Cavett Boatwright family reunion at the Saline County Fairgrounds near Stone Fort. On those occasions, we would mostly stay on a night or three at Aunt Myrtle and Uncle Elroy's in Carterville, just off Crab Orchard Lake. During those many wonderful summer visits, we younger ones from up North took easily to frog spearing and fishing and tree climbing with Mavis and Charlie and Jesse and Dean and

Beaner. And like our folks before, we eventually took to corresponding with one another a few times a year about the various goings on among those we knew in common.

And that more or less explains how I happen to come to know so much about Jolly, who is cousin Mavis's boy, in conjunction with her husband Nevill Rainy from Arkansas. Four years ago, I received a letter from Mavis bringing me up to date as to the goings-on of the jewel of her eye and light of her life — one Michael Allen Edward Rainy, known to everyone except Mavis and his third grade teacher, Miss Archer, as Jolly.

The election of Mr. William Jefferson Clinton to the Presidency of these United States that fateful day in November 1992 had put an irremovable smile to the face of Jolly, Mavis wrote. After all those years of waitin' for the right thing to come along, of bouncing from unsatisfactory job experience to unhappy entrepreneurial venture, he knew, just knew in his heart of hearts, that a New Age had dawned.

Jolly and his old friend Orville Roadhand had come up with a Jim Dandy of an idea that very election night. Orville, you see, is a second cousin twice removed of Jenny Rodour, who is a twice removed cousin of Ms. Hillary Rodham Clinton on her grandaddy's uncle's side. Their idea was so wonderful they could not believe it still made sense the day after the night before in Billy Bob's Basement Bar and Barbecue. It was simplicity at its very best: Of the 2,350,725 residents of the Wonder State of Arkansas, only a few would be going to work for the "Don't Stop Thinkin' About Tomorrow" administration of Mr. W.J. Clinton. Which, of course, meant that a good many of the Northerners who would be on his staff, as well as those who live in the general vicinity of Washington, D.C., were going to need lessons in such nuances of Speakin' Southern as the pronouncing of words like "pecan" (paycon) "dog" (dawg) and "hog" (hawg) — as well as learning to shout "Woooo-Pig-Sueee!!!" correctly without their red plastic "root hog" hats falling off. Of course, knowing the truly professional suck-up skills that come standard with these folks, they figured it would not be much of a retraining effort but more of an informational-type seminar.

So Jolly and Orville incorporated in the state of Delaware as the "Talkin' Southern Seminar Company" and went to teaching people with names like William Wagner Price III that phrases like "He's finally gettin to shell down the corn" translates to "He has concluded being obtuse and is getting to the point of the discussion," and that "Fixin to carry Maw to the Piggly Wiggly" meant about the same as "Preparing to drive Mater into the city for lunch at 21 and shopping."

For awhile, the seminar idea worked like a dream, including the plentiful sales of accompanying posters, coffee mugs, T-shirts, and such.

But one day Talkin Southern Seminars, Inc. was denied preferred vendor status by the Quality and Service Seminars Standard Committee of the Vice President's Task Force on Government Regulations and Procedure Simplification — on the grounds that the company did not meet the minority employment criteria. Orville, who is one-quarter Shawnee on his Daddy's side, claimed that his Native American credentials ought to qualify, since that makes the company fully one-eigth minority-owned and operated. The bureaucrat person they dealt with, however, was adamant that unless one or the other of them staked a claim to being gay, or they quickly hire a woman, they would never meet the guidelines as set forth in the Procedures and Paperwork Simplification Act of 1993, subsection seven, paragraph three.

So Jolly and Orville were forced to put the seminar operations on hold for awhile.

The Pinball Wizard Institute of Advanced Automobile Salesmanship on Inspiration Creek

In the meantime, needing to make ends meet, Jolly went on to work as assistant associate director of quality at Uncle Hector's chicken processing plant just outside Paragould, AR. His specific assignments: teaching statistical process control, Plan-Do-Check-Act and quality function deployment to the pluckers and truckers. Jolly was also assigned an integral role on the Reengineering Process Task Force, in charge specifically of consolidating the pre-gutting and pin feather functions and so forth. He sure enough ended up saving Uncle Hector a bushel-basket full of money.

Now you would think that would have made Jolly feel pretty good, as he was for the first time having a genuine impact on the result of a business. And it did — up to a point. That point being where Sammy Paul made it clear that the folks on the Reengineering Process Task Force were to be looking for new jobs once the work of the task force was over.

Since the Task Force was primarily composed of Sammy Paul, Jolly and Turk Benson — who had semi-retired anyway — and Sammy Paul already had exclusive title to the job of first son, Jolly was the main one in search of a new position. This fell pretty hard on him, as the Task Force had done its job real good, eliminating most of the appealing and high-paid jobs — such as quality training coordinator, salary and wages manager (now made a part of the job of the personnel director's secretary), and safety director. What that left in jobs without a current occupant were two: entrails disposition specialist and sweat band & rubber glove recycler.

But just as Jolly was beginning to almost think about worrying about his future, he received a telephone call from old Orville. Seems Orville had just sold the Talkin' Southern business off to a Lebanese gentleman who had been contracted by a group of Middle Eastern businessmen to help them figure out how to do business with the new crowd in Washington.

Suddenly, the boys were in pretty tall cotton. Never ones to let the kudzu grow under their feet, Jolly and Orville used the proceeds to dive right back into the search for their next venture. Their enthusiasm was ignited through the courtesy of an article Jolly had asked someone to read to him from *The*

Wall Street Journal about Mr. John Rock, the top person of the Oldsmobile division of the General Motors Corporation. Mr. Rock is a down-home boy considered a maverick in the automobile world in that he wears cowboy boots and not always a tie, and is in charge of creating some sorta cultural revolution at the company.

As Jolly and Orville tell it, Mr. Rock's means of reinventing the Oldsmobile company had to do with ordering everyone who worked for the company to this field across the road from the new Saturn factory in Springhill, TN. There they were expected to fall backwards off the tops of telephone poles — I'm not making this up — and wear blindfolds during lunch and hug each other a lot and shout, "We're number one," even though they aren't. In other words, it was a lot like they were all trying out for the A-men corner of the Nicene Baptist Church of Walnut Grove.

The boys were in pretty tall cotton after selling Talkin' Southern Inc. to a Lebanese businessman who wanted to figure out how to do business with the Clinton crowd.

But that is not the how of it. Not by a long shot. In the same newspaper, on the same day, Jolly also read this story about this English lad who had his life changed from playing pinball machines. Now that may not at first seem so much, but this boy, as the story goes, was blind and deaf and speechless, and despite all that became the championship person of pinball in all the country of England. And on top of that, he was cured of his physical challengings during the contest. It is such a famous story in that country that someone even went and wrote a musical play about it. Well Jolly, knowing an opportunity when someone reads it to him, has put two and two together, and along with Orville went out and founded the Pinball Wizard Institute of Advanced Automobile Salesmanship on Inspiration Creek, AR.

This was not as hard an idea to turn into reality as it may first seem. First off, owing to the efficiencies Jolly had come up with as a member of Sammy Paul's reengineering task force, the little pecan grove down by Strangler's Creek Reservoir was about to be idled and put into the Federal Land Bank program. Jolly and Sammy Paul had this economist from the university figure it out, and sure enough, putting the grove away from production is more profitable than harvesting and selling the crop. And as it happens, this same said piece of acreage has always been a favorite place of locals for holding late night snipe hunts. Second, there was already housing of sorts on the creek, built for the convenience of the seasonal laborers who worked in the chicken plant. And as Orville had astutely observed during his research into these kinds of out-of-doors training operations, the worse the accommodations, the more attendees seem to get out of the sessions — and the more they was willing to pay for it.

Thirdly, and the ace in the hole here, was Orville's second cousin Beaty (short for Beatrice) from his daddy's side. Beaty and her husband, Mathew Roy Jenkins, who was lately retired from being a master sergeant of the U.S.

Air Force, were at liberty and had just the perfect credentials to staff and conduct the day-to-day business of the Institute on Inspiration Creek. Over Mathew Roy's 20 years in the Air Force supervising the repair of enlisted personnel fitness and recreation equipment, he had become pretty well-versed in pinball machine repair. Beaty, on the other hand, had for many years been a whiz at holding house parties and selling plastic food containers to the other wives on various bases where they resided. Along the way, she has accumulated just a wonderfully impressive treasury of those inspirational and motivational training and icebreaker activities like, "Stick the straw through the potato" and "How many ways can you think of for using a brick in 60 seconds?" that can be used to show the importance of individual stick-to-it-ness and teamwork.

The main act, however, was not walking on hot coals or falling backwards into your co-workers' arms — though these are interestin' extra credit activities there. The main act at Inspiration Creek Institute, right after the blindfolded pinball machine exercises, was the smoking out and burlap-bag catching of rattlesnakes, which can regularly be seen sunning on the northwest bank of the creek. The catching of rattlesnakes around there is no big deal. Heck, it is regularly practiced by the faithful of Reverend LeRoy Passion's Congregation of the Unquestionable Faith, who annually do this to prove their steadfastness in their beliefs — and

> As anyone knows, when business is good there is just no earthly reason to continue to train people.

to get shown on the TV news. But to Northerners and city folk, the catchin' of a snake by hand is a mind-concentrating experience, and a memorable feat. Much more so than talking directly to Eleanor Roosevelt's ghost.

There was, of course, almost instantaneous early interest in the curriculum of the Institute — particularly the snake catching and team building aspects, owing to the story in USA Today about the planned attendance by Ms. Roseanne Barr and Mr. Adam "Batman" West. But it seems the Hollywood bunch mostly wanted to take the rubber raft trip over to Whitewater and, of course, show their support for the state of Arkansas. Though most of 'em actually tried at one time or another to get to come for free, as they are Friends Of You-Know-Who, Jolly just told 'em they'd have to pay to get the full effect — or hold one of them high dollar dinners for him.

But in the long run, Mavis writes, the Institute has not been able to attract the kind of support from the Detroit automobile manufacturers that had been predicted, once all the movie people tapered off. A consultant, Toni Big Teeth from Taos, NM, who specializes in setting up these sorts of seminars for business, has speculated that this is owed to the fact that the smokin' and catchin' of rattlesnakes is not nearly as photogenic as those "ropes and ladders" courses like the ones they hold over at the Saturn plant.

Personally, I believe the poor results have more to do with the fella from Toyota who was bit on the backside by a coppermouth in the hot springs mineral bath, and talked about it to that 48 hours TV program. That, and the fact that the automobile companies are doing great and as anybody knows, when business is good, there is just no earthly reason to continue training people. Of course, we know that's just so much corn-drinkin' thinkin', but that's the way of it today.

The true fact, of course, is somethin' different. Money comin' in the door was not the deal — it was the money going out that caused the problem. Specifically, the cash flow problem began when Orville and Sherry Lynn Flowers, who was the Institute's treasurer, one day disappeared — along with the treasury itself — and have only been heard from via postal card showing scenes of people in bikini suits on a beach somewhere, possibly Argentina.

Now that dearly did cripple up operations to no end.

Jolly's Last Jam

But down is not out. Not nearly. Jolly has "failed forward" so many times now that he has become a natural born symbol of hope for the likes of himself. That is, people who try and fail and try again and fail again at The Great American Dream of getting rich quick by either (a) starting a no-money down, no-IQ-needed business or (b) repackaging common sense and decades-old advice in books and speeches called "8 Ways To Make People Believe You're Telling Them Something They Don't Already Know."

Even as we sit here jawin', Jolly is out there in Salt Lake City talkin' with that fella who wrote that book about the habits of "7 Annoyingly Successful People" about starting a Southeastern version of his positive habit-building school. And knowin' Jolly, there could even wind up a merger between the Baptists and the Mormons as a result, and wouldn't that beat all?

In the meantime, Jolly is back out there on the speaking circuit. Thanks to his appearing on "The Price is Right" and "Wheel of Fortune" TV shows in the same week, he is almost as famous as someone who plays a doctor on television, but who is not. In addition, he has submitted two new world records to the Guiness Book of World Records people — the world's largest collection of catfish photographs and longest time spent juggling a ping-pong ball on the chin. If you are amazed at this, you should not be. As Jolly himself explained it to me, "Well sir, what do people most admire and envy in this country? It's bein' on TV, winning all kinds of money for doing very little, and bein' famous for no real reason at all."

But his real ace-in-the hole, Jolly confided, is a possible appearance on "The American Gladiators" show. "If I can win me a couple of rounds, maybe even be a runner-up in the semifinals, why, people would respect that even more than me knowin' exactly where Whitewater is," he told me.

So fear not friends, the lad is doin' OK, and is still even money in my book to become one of those household names like Kellogg or Ford or even Forrest Gump.

As for me, I'll keep you posted on the more interestin' parts of this adventure, but for now, *I gotta run...* ∎

RECOMMENDED RESOURCES FOR TRAINERS

MAIL ORDERS TO:
LAKEWOOD BOOKS
50 S. Ninth Street, Minneapolis, MN 55402
800-707-7769 or 612-333-0471
Or fax your order to 612-340-4819.

UNCONDITIONAL GUARANTEE
Examine and use any of the resources on this form for a full 30 days. If you are not completely satisfied, for any reaon whatsoever, simply return and receive a full refund of the purchase price.

Please send me the following publications:

Qty.	Title	$ Amount
_____	Adult Learning in Your Classroom. $24.95	_____
_____	Evaluating Training's Impact. $24.95	_____
_____	Delivering Training: Mastery in the Classroom. $24.95	_____
_____	The Best of Creative Training Techniques. $24.95	_____
_____	Creative Training Techniques Handbook, Vol. 2. By Bob Pike. $49.95	_____
_____	Managing the Front-End of Training. By Bob Pike. $14.95.	_____
_____	Motivating Your Trainees. By Bob Pike. $14.95.	_____
_____	Optimizing Training Transfer. By Bob Pike. $14.95.	_____
_____	TRAINING Magazine. 12 issues/yr. $78 U.S., $88 Canada, $99 Other Int'l.	_____
_____	Creative Training Techniques Newsletter. 12 issues/yr. $99 U.S., $109 Canada, $119 Other Int'l.	_____
_____	Training Directors' Forum Newsletter. 12 issues/yr. $118 U.S., $128 Canada,$138 Other Int'l.	_____
_____	The Lakewood Report on Technology for Learning Newsletter. 12 issues/yr $195 U.S.; $205 Canada; $215 Other Int'l.	_____

SUBTOTAL   Subtotal: _____

In Canada add 7% GST #123705485 (applies to all products)   **Add GST:** _____

In MN add 7% sales tax; in WI add 5% sales tax (does not apply to newsletters)   **Add Tax:** _____

Add $4 for first book; $3 each additional book for shipping & handling.   **Add S&H:** _____

TOTAL   **Total Enclosed:** _____

❏ Check or money order is enclosed. Check payable to Lakewood Publications.
(U.S. Funds on a U.S. Bank)
❏ Please charge:
   ❏ VISA   ❏ MasterCard   ❏ American Express   ❏ Discover
   Card # _____ Exp. ___/___ Signature _____
                                  (Required for Credit Card Use)
NAME_____
TITLE _____
COMPANY_____
ADDRESS (No P.O. Boxes)_____
CITY/STATE/ZIP_____
PHONE (___) _____ FAX (___) _____

H701